D1481576

PROSPECTS FOR THE WEST

*The William L. Clayton Lectures for 1962–63*

*The Fletcher School of Law and Diplomacy*

# Prospects for the West

## By J. WILLIAM FULBRIGHT

UNITED STATES SENATOR FROM ARKANSAS

CHAIRMAN OF THE SENATE COMMITTEE
ON FOREIGN RELATIONS

HARVARD UNIVERSITY PRESS

CAMBRIDGE, MASSACHUSETTS | 1963

# THE WILLIAM L. CLAYTON LECTURES ON
## INTERNATIONAL ECONOMIC AFFAIRS
## AND FOREIGN POLICY

THE FLETCHER SCHOOL of Law and Diplomacy is a graduate school of international affairs, founded in 1933 at Tufts University, Medford, Massachusetts, and administered by Tufts with the cooperation of Harvard University.

The William L. Clayton Center for International Economic Affairs was established at the Fletcher School in 1952 in recognition of Mr. Clayton's services as one of the country's leading business-statesmen and its first Under Secretary of State for Economic Affairs (1946–1948). He is founder, retired head, and currently a director of Anderson, Clayton & Company, the world's largest cotton merchants. The establishment of the Clayton Center was sponsored by the American Cotton Shippers Association; and some two hundred individuals, business firms, banks, and foundations joined in contributing the endowment.

The program of the Clayton Center includes research projects, the William L. Clayton Professorship of International Economic Affairs, the Clayton Fellowships to assist outstanding young men and women to prepare for careers in international economic affairs and diplomacy, the William L. Clayton Latin American Fellowships, and the annual Clayton Lectures.

The lectures were inaugurated in October 1957 by former Secretary of State Dean Acheson. The sixth lecturer in the series, Senator Fulbright, delivered his lectures on April 20 and 30 and May 1, 1963, during the Thirtieth Anniversary Year celebration of the Fletcher School. The Clayton Lectures to date are as follows:

*Power and Diplomacy*
Dean Acheson (1957–58)

*Diplomacy in the Nuclear Age*
Lester B. Pearson (1958–59)

*The Diplomacy of Economic Development*
Eugene R. Black (1959–60)

*European Economic Integration and the Western Alliance*
Paul-Henri Spaak (1960–61)

*United Europe: Challenge and Opportunity*
Walter Hallstein (1961–62)

*Prospects for the West*
J. William Fulbright (1962–63)

# PREFACE

FOR four hundred years prior to the outbreak of the First World War, the history of the world was largely the history of Western civilization, of its dynamism and creativity, of its internal bonds and dissensions, and of its impact on the rest of the world. As a result of the great conflicts of the twentieth century, the West has lost the preponderance of power which, before 1914, had made its ideas and interests and institutions pre-eminent throughout the world. Now, for the first time in modern history, the power and interests of the Western nations are seriously challenged from outside; and it is no longer possible, if it ever was, for the West to regard its ideas and values as having immediate universal applicability. This great historic change is the major factor in the prospects for the West in the second half of the twentieth century.

It is the purpose of these essays to suggest certain directions of Western policy which seem appropriate for the world conditions of our time. I have confined myself to general observations in three major areas which I believe to have bearing on the future of the free societies of the West: their relations with the Soviet Union, their efforts to forge new bonds of unity with each other, and the internal problems of the United States as the leader of the Western community.

The general theme of this book is that the future of the

Western nations depends more on the shaping of their own community and on the character and quality of their own free societies than on their confrontations with those who threaten them from outside. It is neither possible nor desirable under the conditions of our time to impose by direct action the ideas and values of Western democracy on the Communist world or even on the turbulent emerging societies of Asia, Africa, and Latin America. A universal victory for democratic values is clearly beyond the reach of our generation. If ever such a victory comes within reach, it will come, I believe, not through acts of foreign policy, and certainly not of military policy, but rather through the magnetism of freedom itself. The prospects for freedom depend ultimately on how it is practiced in free societies.

.    .    .

I am indebted to a number of persons for assistance and advice in the preparation of my William L. Clayton Lectures, on which these essays are based. Among these I am especially obligated to Seth P. Tillman and John H. Yingling of the staff of the Senate Committee on Foreign Relations. Stephen S. Rosenfeld, Soviet affairs analyst of the *Washington Post,* offered valuable comments and criticisms on the chapter on "Russia and the West." Sidney Hyman, distinguished author and journalist, made a number of valuable suggestions for the chapter on "The American Agenda." Joe W. Fleming of my staff made several suggestions which were incorporated into the text. Max Hall of Harvard University Press, who assisted me twenty years ago in the preparation of the "Fulbright Resolution" when I was a freshman Congressman, edited the text with a fine eye for consistency and detail and improvements of style. I am grateful to Mrs. Elaine Parker for her skillful efforts in the collection and organization of bibliographical materials and in the typing of the earlier drafts.

I very much appreciate having had the opportunity to deliver the William L. Clayton Lectures on April 29–30 and May 1, 1963, and I wish to thank Dean Robert B. Stewart and the faculty of the Fletcher School of Law and Diplomacy for their invitation. I alone am responsible for any errors in fact or judgment in these essays.

J. WILLIAM FULBRIGHT

July 24, 1963

# CONTENTS

# PROSPECTS FOR THE WEST

# 1 · RUSSIA AND THE WEST

HISTORY—or, at any rate, the interpretations that men place upon it—tends as much to obscure as to clarify when applied to the present and the future. The lessons of the past are rarely lessons of simple and direct analogy, because the affairs of men rarely if ever unfold more than once in identical sequence, combination, and context. In its efforts to cope with the Soviet challenge, the West, I think, has too often devised its policies in terms of facile, and misleading, analogies with the conflicts of the past, tending at times to perceive identity of motive and design where there is only similarity in appearance or detail. The Soviet challenge to the Western world is in some respects similar to Germany's two bids for world hegemony, but in other respects it is quite different, confronting the West with new kinds of problems for which the "lessons" of Munich or Versailles are of little relevance and may well be misleading.

The minds of men are cluttered with ideas, and illusions, about the past. Some of the most grievous errors in the diplomacy of World War II, such as the policy—or non-policy—of "unconditional surrender," were based on misconceptions about the diplomacy of World War I, or events of our own Civil War, and, similarly, some of the gravest mistakes of recent years have been rooted in erroneous or oversimplified ideas about the 1930's and 1940's. History does not "repeat itself." Its uses for the present and the future are not in the form of simple and literal analogies, but rather in its broad indications of the kinds of human effort that are likely to be useful and the kinds that are likely to fail; in its empirical distinctions between the desirable and the possible; and most of all, perhaps, in its suggestions as to the limits as well as the possibilities of human capacity.

If there is any single lesson in the history of nations that can profitably be brought to bear on the problems of our own time, it is that we must be cautious in our prescriptions and modest in our aspirations, not because grand designs and universal ideas are undesirable in the abstract, but because they are desirable only in the abstract, far exceeding the demonstrated limits of human capacity and human wisdom. The Communists, of course, with their messianic ideology, are far more in need of instruction in this proposition than are the Western democracies, but the West too, sporadically, has been fired by lofty aspirations quite out of balance with the limitations of its human and material resources.

．　　　．　　　．

BECAUSE of the vast discrepancy between Communist ideology and historic reality, we can, I think, be quite certain that Communism as Marx and Lenin conceived it will not prevail in the world. It will not prevail because it is at variance with the real world and could only be brought about by the one kind of revolution it is incapable of precipitating, a revolution in the nature of man. Men and nations, however, are often moved not by what is true but by what they *believe* to be true. In this sense, it is not Communism that challenges the free world but the misconceptions which Communism fosters, of which the most dangerous is its claim to universal validity. The task of Western policy, therefore, is not directly to destroy Communism as an ideology—an enterprise which the erosions of time and history rather than acts of statecraft will accomplish— but to demonstrate the futility and danger of its misconceptions, while our major energies are dedicated to the strengthening and improvement of our own society.

Ideas are the prisons of idealogues, a rule to which the Communists are no exception. "From enthusiasm to imposture," wrote Gibbon, "the step is perilous and slippery; the demon of Socrates affords a memorable instance how a wise man may deceive himself, how a good man may deceive others, how the conscience may slumber in a mixed and middle state between self-illusion and voluntary fraud."[1]

The devolution of Communist ideology from "enthusiasm" to "imposture" reflects the growing divergence between a stagnant idea and an evolving reality. Communism in its classical form represented a response to the brutal upheavals and abuses of the industrial revolution in its early stages. Marx's manifesto, however, became a quasi-religion and a mover of events in its own right. Unchanged in their broad assumptions and tenets in over a hundred years, the basic ideas of Communism have become increasingly divorced from the realities of modern Western industrial society, holding their adherents, nonetheless, in an intellectual prison in which observed facts are rejected or distorted to fit the specifications of a specious doctrine.

It is not necessary here to rehearse the tenets of Marxist-Leninist theory and the specific ways in which history,

3

indeed Soviet history itself, has proven them wrong. In its explanations of the forces and movements of the modern world, Communist theory is easily shown to be unsound. It was not in the advanced industrial states that Communist revolutions occurred but in backward countries like Russia and China, where revolutions were bred by war-weariness, the land hunger of the peasants, and other factors which had little if anything to do with capitalism as a form of economic organization. Traditional Western colonialism, which Marxist theory attributed to a desperate struggle for markets, was in fact motivated far more by considerations of strategy and prestige than by economics. The great wars of the twentieth century had virtually nothing to do with economic rivalry, as the Communists professed to believe, and everything to do with the passions of modern nationalism.

Since the end of World War II the gap between Communist ideology and the real world has grown wider still. The Western nations have relinquished all but a few vestiges of their colonial empires while surging forward in the development of mass consumption economies within their own borders. In addition, the Western democracies, instead of falling ever deeper into mutual hostility as Communist doctrine predicts, have created and sustained a viable alliance and have made considerable, albeit inadequate, progress in the fields of economic and political collaboration.

The success of Communism as a revolutionary force in the world is not the product of its fundamentally defective doctrine but rather the result of the impact and example of the Soviet state, which, through discipline, hard work, and

4

the forcible exaction of great sacrifices from its people, converted backward Russia into a powerful modern industrial society in the span of a single generation. The defectiveness of Communist theory, however, in no way implies that the leaders of Russia and China are not motivated by its tenets in the shaping of national policy. The important factor here is not the validity or invalidity of doctrine but the fact that it is *believed* to be valid by the men who have power in the Communist world.

There is every reason to think that the men who rule Russia today are no less persuaded than were Lenin and Trotsky of the validity of Communism, of the universality of its mission, and of the inevitability of its triumph. Khrushchev, so far as I am able to gauge his character, manages to be both ideologue and opportunist, a narrow-minded mystic in his view of the world and its destiny and a practical realist in devising tactics for guiding human destiny along its preordained course. I see no reason to question the sincerity of his conviction in such pronouncements as the following: "No magicians or witches will ever revive the dying capitalist system. Capitalism is going to be buried. Only the new is growing. This is the law of life."[2]

An impressive amount of scholarship has been dedicated in recent years to exploring the bases of Soviet foreign policy, with a view to determining the relative significance of ideology on the one hand and of Russian national interest on the other. Much of this analysis has rested on a tacit assumption that the Russians are quite clear in their own minds on this theoretical distinction—an assumption which I am not at all certain is valid. Nationalism, both Russian nationalism and that of the underdeveloped countries, has

5

certainly intruded itself into Soviet policy, but more, I think, as a powerful conditioning factor than as an admitted change of direction. Soviet policy, like our own, has its matrix in human minds, wherein reason and emotion, hopes and memories, ideas and prejudices combine and interact in ways that do not readily submit to precise and measurable distinctions. The motives of Soviet policy, in short, are a synthesis of ideological conviction, historical conditioning, rational calculation, irrational fears and hopes, and personal predilections—which is to say, they are obscure.

More productive, I think, and more useful than the exploration of Soviet motives is an effort to determine the character and methods of Soviet strategy. It is the fact rather than the motivation of Communist imperialism that directly concerns us, and it is the methods which it employs that bear upon the shaping of our own policy. If the West is successfully to thwart the Communist dream of universal empire, it is less important for us to know *why* the Soviet leaders wish to "bury" us than to know *how* they propose to do it. It is very clear that they do not intend to leave the process to the mystical force of history, however "inevitable" its outcome. They are going to help the process along with all of their resources and it is the task of Western statesmen to estimate what those resources are, the way in which they have been used in the past, and how they are likely to be used in the future.

There is nothing in either Communist theory or Soviet practice to suggest a propensity for suicidal risks. "The theory of the inevitability of the eventual fall of capitalism," wrote George Kennan some years ago, "has the fortunate connotation that there is no hurry about it. The forces of

6

progress can take their time in preparing the final *coup de grace*."[3]

The fact that the Soviets usually pursue their aims with caution is at least as important in its implications for the West as the fact that these aims are unlimited. It means in effect that the pursuit of ultimate goals is circumscribed in time and scope by consideration of feasibility. Soviet estimations of feasibility, of course, may be wrong, as they were in the Korean War and the Cuban crisis of 1962, but for the most part they have not been wrong. When the West has acted with both patience and firmness, it has usually been rewarded by Soviet prudence.

It is in this respect that efforts to apply the "lessons" of German aggression in the 1930's and 1940's to the Soviet imperialism of our own time in terms of literal and simple analogies are likely to lead us into serious errors about the character of Soviet policy. It is often said that the mistake of the West in treating Hitler as a normal politician was a profound blunder which should not be repeated in our dealings with the Soviet Union. This is beyond question, but it does not follow that the kinds of Western response which might have contained German aggression in the thirties provide us with a blueprint for containing Soviet expansion in our own time. There is no "norm" of abnormality, and although Stalin was probably as abnormal a man as Hitler, he was abnormal in quite different ways, to say nothing of the different conditions and circumstances in which he operated.

Neither Stalin nor his successors have exhibited anything like the suicidal mania of Hitler's Germany, a fact which in certain respects is reassuring to the West but which in other

7

respects makes the Soviet Union a far more formidable antagonist than was Nazi Germany. The distinction was explained by Stalin himself, who, in a conversation with Anthony Eden in December 1941, commented that Hitler was a very able man whose one mistake was that he did not know when to stop. Eden reacted with amused skepticism and Stalin said: "You are smiling and I know why you are smiling. You think that if we are victorious I shall not know when to stop. You are wrong. I shall know!"[4]

Beyond the fact that both Nazi Germany and Soviet Russia were powerful and aggressive nations, there is little in the experience of the West in relation to Hitler's Germany to guide us in our dealings with the Soviet Union. Hitler, as his biographer has put it, was a man "without aims," which is to say, without rational, tractable aims. After a point he broke through the barriers of feasibility, violating a cardinal rule of politics by ceasing to relate his ambitions to his capacity to realize them. In so doing, he plunged the world into war but under conditions that made his ultimate defeat inevitable. The Russians, on the other hand, whose ambitions are, if anything, greater in scope than those of Nazi Germany, have nonetheless exhibited no such instinct for self-destruction. Whatever their missionary zeal, it has never beclouded their determination to proceed with practical caution, a quality which, even in the complete absence of scruples, makes their aims limited in practice.

The implication of this for the West, I think, is that although the Russians are unlikely to plunge the world into nuclear war so long as their leadership retains the capacity for rational calculation which it has thus far displayed, neither are they likely to commit fatal blunders of judgment

8

which will lead to their defeat and destruction. It is in this respect that the Soviet Union is an immediately less dangerous but ultimately more formidable adversary for the West than was Nazi Germany.

It is scarcely productive, under these circumstances, for the free world to try to shape its policies on the basis of recondite speculations about the ultimate goals of the Soviet leaders. It is far more rewarding for the West, however hard it may be on the nerves, to continue to concentrate its energies on making Communist expansion unfeasible and on multiplying the conditions in which the Soviets will be compelled to play the game of international relations by the traditional rules. How they square the necessity to adjust to political realities with their Marxian conscience is their affair, not ours.

Patience, circumspection, and flexibility are qualities which are not at all incompatible with Communist ideology or with the Russian temperament. When confronted with intractable obstacles or superior force, the Soviets, like their tsarist predecessors, have retreated in good order, rebuilt their forces, and awaited favorable opportunities to restore their fortunes. Examples of this propensity come readily to mind: Lenin's "New Economic Policy" of the 1920's, which was in fact a retreat from initial and unsuccessful experiments with Communism; Stalin's policy in the inter-war years of "socialism in one country" and his abandonment in the early postwar years, in the face of Western resolve, of Soviet incursions on Iran and Greece; and, more recently, Khrushchev's policy of "peaceful coexistence" coming in the wake of the failure of Stalin's more direct and brutal methods.

9

Soviet tactical flexibility is thus a highly relevant factor for the West in the shaping of its own policies, but it must never be forgotten that the complement of restraint is an unerring opportunism, a constant probing for opportunities to expand Soviet power wherever it can be done without excessive risk. The invasion of South Korea in 1950 is of course the classic example of Soviet boldness in a situation in which the West permitted its own intentions to be misinterpreted. In other instances, notably the continuing Soviet pressure on Berlin, Western determination and clarity as to its intentions have been rewarded by Soviet prudence. The lesson of Korea and Berlin, and of Cuba as well, is that the West can count upon Soviet moderation and restraint to the extent, and only to the extent, that the West is absolutely clear in keeping the Soviets informed about where caution must be observed. This in turn requires Western leaders to be absolutely clear in their own minds as to the boundaries of Western interests.

Underlying the vagaries and circumlocutions of Soviet policy is a profound hostility to the West which must also be a factor in our policy calculations. Soviet hostility to the West is not primarily a product of fear and resentment of Western attitudes toward Communism. It is rooted more in theory than experience and is directed less at the behavior of Western countries than at the nature of their society. This cannot be equated with Western fear and dislike of Soviet Communism which is essentially a reaction to Soviet behavior and Soviet aims. "In thirty years' experience with Soviet official literature," writes Kennan, "I cannot recall an instance of a non-Communist government being credited with a single generous or worthy impulse."[5]

Though fundamentally different in motive and nature, Russian hostility to the West and Western hostility to Russia nonetheless feed upon each other, generating distortions of view on both sides. The Soviets, and we, to a lesser extent, suffer in viewing each other from the misrepresentations of a "mirror image," as one psychologist has put it, a "discrepancy between the real and the perceived."[6] It is not that the popular American view of the Soviet Union is false but that it is at least to some degree and in some instances a distortion or exaggeration of the truth. Perceiving the outside world through the prism of our own moral values, we Americans are inclined to interpret our perceptions of the outside world in terms of absolute good and absolute evil, rejecting the ambiguities and uncertainties that somehow make us uncomfortable. The Soviets in turn, indoctrinated with a primitive "demon" theory of capitalist societies, perceive the West through a prism of fear, suspicion, and theoretical delusion.

The conditions and character of the Soviet-Western dialogue have tended over the years to reinforce the "mirror image" between the two societies. The missionary and crusading spirit of conflicting ideologies has injected itself into diplomacy, displacing the traditional methods of quiet and courteous exchange with a new vocabulary of epithets and accusations, publicly exchanged. Under these conditions, diplomacy ceases to be a morally neutral method for conducting business and becomes itself a weapon of ideological conflict. Compromise and accommodation, the virtues of the old diplomacy, become reprehensible, and even treasonable, under the new diplomacy.

Confronting each other in full public view, both Soviet

and Western statesmen have all too often used the negotiating forum to address not each other but their own national constituencies and the larger constituency of world public opinion. This makes for excellent propaganda but has not proven conspicuously productive of agreements on outstanding issues. Subjected to the transitory forces of public emotion, the diplomat is under the strongest pressure to strike postures rather than bargains, to reinforce the prejudices and preconceptions of the "mirror image." Or if there is a strong public push for some kind of agreement or "success," the negotiator is likely to take refuge in imprecision, coming to an ostensible agreement that obscures but does not resolve existing differences. There comes to mind, in this connection, the ephemeral agreements with the Russians in the 1950's—the "spirit of Geneva" which ended with the suppression of the Hungarian Revolution, and the "spirit of Camp David" which ended with the U-2 affair.

The nuclear test ban negotiations in Geneva afford a striking example of the mischief wrought by excessive publicity and political comment on the day-to-day conduct of negotiations. The question of how many inspections a year will provide adequate guarantees against cheating is not a political one but a technical one requiring highly sophisticated scientific evaluation. It is, therefore, difficult to understand how it is that many Americans, including members of Congress, who do not claim expert knowledge in this field, have come to hold such fervent opinions on the appropriate number of inspections. Some of these critics accuse our negotiators of "surrendering to Communism" if they make concessions to the Soviet position while others charge them with "being against peace" if they do not. Such uninformed criticism contributes nothing to the search for a workable

agreement; on the contrary, it impedes the effort by sub-
jecting our negotiators to political pressures that have little
if any relevance to the task at hand.

I believe that the prospects for success in these negotiations would be enhanced if they were removed from the
arena of cold war invective and entrusted to quiet and con-
fidential negotiation by professional diplomats.* The time
for public debate comes after, and not before, an accord
has been reached, at which time a basic policy decision has
to be made, not by diplomats but by the elected representatives of the people.

Unlike the test ban negotiations, the discussion of
"general and complete disarmament" is, in my opinion, an
exercise in cold war fantasy, a manifestation of the decep-
tion and pretense of the new diplomacy. In a world
profoundly divided by ideological conflict and national
rivalries—conditions which are almost certain to prevail
for the foreseeable future—it is inconceivable that the
world's foremost antagonists could suddenly and mirac-
ulously dispel their animosities and vest in each other the
profound trust and confidence which "general and complete
disarmament" would require. There is nothing but mischief
in negotiations which no statesman seriously expects to
succeed. They become a forum for the generation of false
hopes and profound disappointments, a cold war battle-
ground for the exchange of epithets and accusations of bad
faith in the face of certain failure. The net result is to reinforce the "mirror image" of mistrust and animosity through
which the two societies see each other.

---

* Since this lecture was given, high-level negotiations in Moscow for
a limited nuclear test ban have succeeded, among other reasons because
of their limited objective.

13

The dangers of the "mirror image" are obvious. It poses an artificial barrier to communication and negotiation and in so doing exacerbates tensions and animosities. If we are to cope successfully with the Soviet challenge to the Western world, we must see the Soviets as they are, no better and no worse. I do not think that this is simply a problem of resolving "misunderstandings." I am quite sure that even the most accurate and unemotional perceptions of the Soviet Union will still reveal a great nation dedicated to the imposition on an unwilling world of its own form of totalitarian society.

It is all the more essential, in these circumstances, that we develop widening channels of communication, of cultural and educational exchange, between the two societies. Man, even Communist man, is not a completely irrational animal, and if he is exposed with sufficient frequency and intensity to realities which do not fit the mold of his predilections and prejudices, one can at least hope that in time he will begin to question them. If we can somehow in the years to come contain the passions and animosities that threaten the world with catastrophe, it is at least possible that the cumulative impact of the real world of experience on the imaginary world of Marxian dogma will gradually bring about profound alterations in Marxian theory, in the character of Soviet society, and in the relations of Russia to the West.

·     ·     ·

SUCH alterations, which can come about only through the evolutionary processes of history, are in fact already well advanced, having begun in 1917 when the Soviet state was born. From the earliest days of their rule the Bolsheviks came up against the fact that the possession and exercise of political power imposes all sorts of necessities on the politician, saddling him, regardless of ideology, with the traditional compulsions of statecraft and national interest. The Bolsheviks quickly learned, though they were loath to admit it, that it was not the world vision of Marx and Lenin that determined their immediate and concrete prospects but the history, the geography, and the human and material resources of the Russian nation. Aside from decisions imposed on them by their own weakness—the tactical retreat from world revolution and the diversion of their energies to the task of building the strength of Russia—the Bolsheviks were subjected to the more profound and permanent intrusion of Russia itself, whose national interest became joined with ideological goals in the minds of the Soviet leaders.

There occurred in Russia during the interwar years a fusion of the two great revolutionary forces of the twentieth century, nationalism and socialism. One perceives in the dreary and heavy-handed official literature of Stalinist Russia the same chauvinism, the same mystic faith in the unique superiority of Russian life and the Russian land, that permeated the political writings of Dostoevsky. Under Stalin, and especially during the Second World War, which the Russians called the "Second Great Fatherland War," the traditional forms and symbols of nationalism were restored to Russian life. No less than Lenin and Stalin before him, Khrushchev is a leader who was shaped and formed by the Russian experience.

Soviet imperialism is a manifestation of expansive nationalism as well as of the ideological drive for world revolution. Increasingly over the years the drive for world-wide socialist revolution has become a drive for Russian hegemony and influence. It is ironical that although the Russian leaders have strongly supported non-Communist governments, such as those of Egypt and India, when it has seemed to suit Russian interests to do so, they have quickly lost enthusiasm for Communist revolutions, however pure their Marxism, when those revolutions have gone beyond the interests of the Soviet state. China, of course, is the prime example of this propensity.

It is this intrusion of nationalism, both in Russia and throughout the world, that has enormously complicated and changed the character of Communism and its drive for world supremacy. Twentieth-century nationalism has proven to be a far more powerful force than classical Communist doctrine foresaw, and, indeed, a far more powerful revolutionary force than Communism itself. Khrushchev's foreign policy has been dedicated in great measure, and with less than striking success, to the task of adjusting Soviet ambitions to the realities of nationalism, both within the Communist world and in the many lands which have achieved nationhood, or national consciousness, in the years since World War II.

The evolution of Soviet policy from Lenin to Stalin to Khrushchev has largely reflected the intrusion of traditional nationalist attitudes upon an internationalist ideology with universal aims. This intrusion has occurred not by conscious design and in measurable quantities as some students of the Soviet Union have suggested, but pragmatically and by evolving stages. Lenin acted at first, but only for a brief period, on the orthodox Marxist assumption that Bolshevism could survive only if the Russian Revolution were followed quickly by revolution in the most advanced industrial countries of Europe, especially Germany. The failure of this universalist policy was quite clear to Stalin, who, at the outset of his rule, came to the practical though unorthodox conclusion that if Communism were to survive it would have to survive, at least for a time, in Russia alone. He proceeded to pursue a policy of "socialism in one country" while attempting to secure Russia against "capitalist encircle-ment" by building up the strength of the Soviet Union and by the expansion of Soviet power into surrounding terri-tories, which were of course the same lands that had historically been coveted by the Russian tsars.

Stalin, whom Milovan Djilas describes as "one of those rare terrible dogmatists capable of destroying nine tenths of the human race to 'make happy' the one tenth,"[7] pursued a foreign policy which reflected an amalgam of traditional Russian national interest, his own hard-headed interpreta-tions of Marxist-Leninist doctrine, and, not least, the megalomania of his own personality. Stalinist policy, both before and after World War II, was motivated by a drive for absolute control, both within Russia and over the satellite empire which Russia acquired as a result of the victory of the Allies in the war. His policy, in short, was one of crude and traditional imperialism. "Everyone," he said in April 1945, "imposes his own system as far as his army can reach. It cannot be otherwise."[8]

Stalin's policy was in some respects a sensible adaptation to objective reality, but "Stalinism," in all its harsh excesses, was the product of a cruel and abnormal personality. Stalin's death, accordingly, marked a decisive turn in Russian history and world politics.

Russia after Stalin underwent something of a psychological revolution, a readjustment of Soviet policy to the realities of the postwar world. The world policy of Khrushchev may be defined in general as an effort to realize the same goals which Stalin pursued but by more subtle means. Free of Stalin's psychotic fears and suspicions, Khrushchev has revised the policy of total belligerency in favor of varied and more sophisticated techniques and combinations of techniques. No less than Stalin's cruder methods, however, Khrushchev's flexible maneuvers of cautious military pressure, summit diplomacy and *détente,* foreign aid and "peaceful coexistence," have had the central objective of weakening and undermining the Western military alliance and the broader system of Western unity.

Under Khrushchev, the obsession with absolute control has given way to a drive for *influence,* wherever promising opportunities for gaining it arise. In effect, this has meant a concerted drive to influence to whatever degree possible the nationalist revolutions which engulf Asia, Africa, and Latin America. With influence rather than total domination as an acceptable short-term goal of Soviet policy, Khrushchev has increasingly resorted to the traditional instruments of foreign policy, such as diplomatic contacts and trade, economic and technical assistance, educational and cultural exchanges. These are instruments relying more on persuasion than coercion, designed to convince non-Communist countries all over the world that it is safe and profitable to do business with the Soviet Union.

Khrushchev, in short, has radically altered Stalin's policy

of expansion into and total domination over adjacent territories. He has in effect revived the universalist policies of Lenin but with methods which are new and unorthodox in Marxian terms. These methods are essentially a skillful and flexible utilization of the enormous new power of the Soviet state. They have carried Soviet influence in varying degrees to distant areas of the world which, while Stalin lived, were beyond the Soviet grasp. Pragmatist an opportunist that he is, Khrushchev, no less than Lenin before him, is caught up in the mystic vision of Marx, a vision of humanity caught up in a force of historic predestiny that transcends human choice. "It is necessary," he writes, "that everybody should understand the irrevocable fact that the historic process is irreversible."[9]

.        .        .

MEANS have a way in human affairs of consuming their ends when the ends, despite continuing and concerted effort, remain distant and unrealized over a long period of time. This is why it seems to me that it is the operating strategy, rather than the theoretical objectives, of Soviet Communism that is of direct relevance for the West in the shaping of its own policies.

It is not beyond the power of the West to encourage the Soviets further along the course toward more moderate and less dangerous methods than those used by Stalin in Korea or by Khrushchev in Cuba. Their own predisposition for caution works in our favor in this respect. There are a number of ways in which the West can encourage Soviet moderation.

First, and most obviously, the West can maintain such

strength that any departure from moderation on the Soviet side would involve unacceptable risks.

Secondly, the West can make it clear to the Soviets at every possible opportunity that it is not Communism which is at issue between the Soviet Union and the West but Communist *imperialism,* and that the Soviet Union, insofar as it renounces expansionist and subversive ambitions, can enjoy a safe and honorable national life without threat or danger from the West.

Thirdly, and most important, the West, through the utilization and unification of its own immense human and material resources, can so strengthen the internal fabric of the free societies as to make them impregnable to external ideological assault and at the same time magnetic examples of social justice and material well-being for the entire world.

It is of course possible that the third of these approaches could have the opposite of a moderating effect. The narrowing of the horizons of Soviet ambition in the face of growing Western strength and unity could conceivably lead irresponsible or incompetent leaders into some desperate gamble to reverse the tide. Or, in tsarist fashion, they might raise new barriers to contact and communication in order to seal off the Russian peoples and the peoples of Eastern Europe from the magnetism of the West, thereby widening the gap between two worlds. We must attempt, therefore, while building the strength and unity of the Atlantic world, to find limited ways of acting directly on the Soviet Union itself, of communicating with the Russian people in such a way as to exert some influence on the development of Soviet society. We must try to convey accurate information to the Russians about Western life, about the aims of Western policy, and about the heavy price that the cold war exacts from both their people and ours. I do not know whether we can influence Russian public opinion and strengthen it as a brake against dangerous and adventurous policies, but I believe that we must try to do this as a matter of responsibility not to the Russians but to ourselves.

In these ways we can encourage Soviet moderation. It is by no means certain, but neither is it inconceivable, that if we are patient and wise and strong in our dealings with the Soviets, we can encourage moderate means to consume immoderate ends, consigning the dream of a world remade in the Soviet image not to destruction by some apocalyptic act, but to a gradual "withering away," to starvation in the thin, dry soil of Marxian illusion.

The one thing about Soviet society and Soviet foreign policy that is very clear is that they are in continuing change and evolution. Those who attribute to the Soviet leaders a permanent, monolithic, and unalterable determination to destroy the free societies of the West are crediting the Soviet Union with an unshakable constancy of will that, so far as I know, no nation has ever before achieved.

I do not pretend to foresee the future course of Soviet policy. I do suggest, however, that the trend over recent years, as evidenced by the rejection of Chinese importunities for a more adventurous policy, has been toward relative moderation by the Russians and that it is within the power of the West to encourage and reinforce this tendency. If it is ingenuous to predict the "mellowing" of Soviet policy, it is equally ingenuous to regard Soviet policy and goals as absolutely intractable. It is certainly possible, although not necessarily probable, that the changes in the character and structure of Soviet society which have occurred since the death of Stalin, such as the abatement of police terror and the development of the Central Committee into a kind of rudimentary parliamentary body, will in turn generate further and more significant changes in Soviet policy.

Powerful forces for change are at work within the Soviet Union. Soviet society and the Soviet economy are becoming highly complex, too complex to be completely controlled by a highly centralized dictatorship. Many of the same factors are at work within Russia as those which over many centuries shaped the evolution of the free societies of the West. Modernization, writes Walter Lippmann, "is changing the character of the Soviet State—changing it from a Byzantine despotism into what might be described as a Western state in the very earliest phases of its development."[10]

. . .

AMONG the changes which have occurred in Soviet relations with the outside world none is more important in its effects on world politics than the fact that Russia is no longer alone in the Communist world. No longer the single monolithic center of power in the Communist bloc, as it was in Stalin's time, Moscow is now confronted with independent centers of power in Peking and, to a much lesser extent, in certain of the less subservient European satellites.

Coalition diplomacy, as the Russians are now learning, is a task for which totalitarian powers are peculiarly ill-equipped. Unschooled in the democratic processes of bargaining and compromise in their internal political life, they are lacking also in the political skills necessary for holding together an international coalition. Communist dogma, moreover, with its emphasis on the infallibility of the Party and the "unshakable unity" of the "socialist camp," further derogates from the capacity of Communist leaders to resolve their differences by compromise and accommodation. According to Communist doctrine, the consequences of the diffusion of power are nothing less than disastrous. "The existence of factions," wrote Stalin, "leads to the existence of a number of centers, and the existence of a number of centers connotes the absence of a common center of the Party, the breaking up of the unity of will, the weakening and disintegration of discipline, the weakening and disintegration of the dictatorship."[11]

The conflict between China and Russia, a product of both national and ideological rivalry, is exacerbated by the rigidities of the Communist mind. Mystics and missionaries do not as a general rule take kindly to heretical ideas about the road to grace. To the fanatical ideologue the heretic is more unspeakable than the avowed enemy and, circumstances permitting, may be dealt with accordingly. Stalin, for example, found it easier to come to terms with Hitler than Trotsky. Tolerance of mind is a democratic quality which is not only lacking in totalitarian societies but is fundamentally incompatible with their very nature. In the light of these considerations, and of the record of Sino-Soviet relations in recent years, it seems probable that the Communist world will not soon or easily resolve its internal differences, and that at such time, if ever, as those differences are resolved, it will be at the price of greater sacrifices in the totalitarian rigidity of orthodox Communist doctrine than can now be contemplated by either Russians or Chinese.

The meaning of all this for the West is considerably less clear. The West can encourage a certain degree of national independence within the Communist world through limited programs of aid and other forms of cooperation with such countries as Poland and Yugoslavia. For the time being, however, I think it would be unwise for the West to try to exert any direct influence on Sino-Soviet relations, which are, after all, deteriorating quite satisfactorily on their own. As Stalin learned—or should have learned—from his policy toward the West, nothing is more effective in restoring the unity of a disheveled alliance than the active intervention of a powerful outside force.

.        .        .

COMMUNISM, it has been said, is not a truly revolutionary force in its own right but rather a "scavenger" of revolutions. In the emerging nations of Asia, Africa, and Latin America, the force that makes revolutions is neither Communism nor Western constitutional democracy, but a virulent nationalism bred by colonialism and by chronic social and economic maladjustments. The West, I think, has largely acknowledged this fact, and though it is hardly delighted with the disinclination of the emergent countries to build their societies in the Western image, it also recognizes that its own aims and interests are not incompatible with the aspiration of the underdeveloped countries to national self-fulfillment. The Russians, on the other hand, though recognizing and seeking with some success to identify themselves with the forces of nationalism, do so for purposes of advancing their own aims, which, being imperialist, are in basic conflict with the nationalist aims of the emergent countries. "Bourgeois

24

nationalism" is regarded as a transitional phase between colonialism and socialism on the Soviet model, a force to be utilized and shaped to ends beyond itself.

The high hopes which the Russians had a few years ago for the expansion of their influence in Asia, Africa, and Latin America have been largely disappointed. Soviet expectations of a decisive breakthrough were based on the illusion that in the wake of Western decolonization the new countries would turn to the Communists for assistance and leadership. In fact the nationalist leaders of the emergent nations have with few exceptions exhibited the same distaste for the Soviet embrace as for that of the former Western colonial powers. Only in Cuba did a nationalist revolution become a Communist revolution. In almost all the other emergent countries nationalist leaders have found it possible and profitable to accept aid from both East and West, while rejecting the domination of either. Neither Communism nor Western democratic capitalism has demonstrated any great magnetic attraction for the new countries. They are instead groping, with varying degrees of success, for their own undoctrinaire roads to political stability and economic development.

The fundamental conflict between Communist imperialism and the nationalism of the emergent nations, already apparent in certain countries which have been recipients of Soviet aid, is likely to become more apparent as memories of Western colonialism fade. Later I shall comment in some detail on the political and economic purposes of Western aid programs. Here it is sufficient to point out that although the aims of the nationalist revolutions of Asia, Africa, and Latin America are profoundly incompatible with the Communist

25

vision of a future world order, they are fundamentally compatible with Western interests. Because of this compatibility, it is within the potential of Western statesmanship to shape a global concert of free nations embracing most of the non-Communist world.

. . .

IN EUROPE as in the former colonial areas, Soviet policy is heavily committed to the goal of dividing the non-Communist world against itself. Having provoked the creation of NATO in the late 1940's, the Soviets have since dedicated their best efforts to the task of bringing about its disruption. The alliance of the great nations of the West is the ultimate and insuperable obstacle to the realization of Communist ambitions. Its destruction, accordingly, is the foremost goal of Soviet strategy. The "standard components" of Soviet success, writes George Kennan, are "one part Soviet resourcefulness and singlemindedness of purpose; two parts amateurism, complacency, and disunity on the part of the West."[12]

I think it is not too much to say that over the last half century the unity or disunity of the West has been the ultimate determinant of the fortunes of Communism. The Bolshevik Revolution of 1917 was made possible, in the final analysis, by the destruction of the old Concert of Europe in a savage war. Communism thereafter was tightly confined within the frontiers of Russia until the Western nations fell upon each other in a second round of savagery, opening the floodgates to Communist expansion beyond Russia's frontiers, culminating in the conquest of China.

In the years since World War II the West has forged sufficient unity to contain the expansive thrust of Communism. If the West goes on to realize its fullest possible strength in an Atlantic partnership, it can, I believe, bring about a decisive shift in the world balance of power and permanently foreclose the possibility of significant Communist expansion. This can be accomplished without direct action on the part of the West toward the Soviet Union but rather as a result of what the West does within its own community. Such a course, requiring thought, foresight, persistence, and self-discipline, is far more difficult but also far more promising than the traditional and relatively simple course of direct action by physical force which appeals so much to the demagogues of the right.

For good and ample reason, the Soviet Union is disturbed and perplexed by the revival of the economic and political strength of Western Europe. In effect, a power vacuum is being filled by the new Europe, putting an end to the conditions which made possible the great expansion of Soviet power in the years immediately following World War II. The success of the European Common Market, the reconciliation of France and Germany, and the possibilities of a broader Atlantic community are developments for which Marxian doctrine can provide neither explanations nor antidotes. The Soviets are confronted with a great and growing new weight on the Western side of the power scale, with no commensurate growth of power on the Eastern side, and their apprehension, I would guess, is greater than they have been willing to admit.

The consummation of this trend, or its reversal, depends

upon whether the West fulfills the promise of unity or becomes divided against itself. This, I believe, is the most important issue in our foreign relations.

The Russians, besides being justifiably concerned over the growth of Western strength and unity, have a somewhat emotional preoccupation with Western Germany, whose potential power, I think, they are inclined to overrate. For obvious historical reasons, the Russians have developed an enormous respect for German efficiency and power. Their fear of Germany, solidly rooted in two German invasions of Russia in a single generation, is a powerful factor in the Soviet determination to keep Germany divided. The recurrent crises over Berlin, it seems to me, are a reflection of a feeling of urgency on the part of the Russians that they must consolidate their control of East Germany before West Germany realizes its full power potential, and especially before West Germany is armed with nuclear weapons. They hope to achieve this by persuading the West to accept a codification of the status quo of a partitioned Germany, and the lever for "persuading" the West is of course Berlin.

Soviet policy toward Germany cannot be understood entirely, or even predominantly, in terms of the expansionist ambitions of the Soviet Union. It stems at least as much from Russia's historic fear of and admiration for German power. Lenin expected at the time of the Bolshevik Revolution that the leadership of world Communism would soon pass from Russia to Germany. Stalin rarely concealed his admiration for German power and efficiency and even attempted, in a miscarriage of statesmanship that matched the Western mistake at Munich, to purchase the safety of Russia by a compact with Nazi Germany. Once, near the end of the war, when someone expressed the view that Germany would be enfeebled for a half a century, Stalin replied: "No, they will recover, and very quickly. That is a highly developed industrial country with an extremely qualified and numerous working class and technical intelligentsia. Give them twelve to fifteen years and they'll be on their feet again."[13] In 1958, Anastas Mikoyan declared: "Were it not for two devastating wars Germany, I think, would be richer than America."[14]

While the recovery of Europe has confronted the Soviets with a new and unexpected weight in the balance of political and economic power, American nuclear superiority has kept the balance of military power favorable to the West. If the Soviets expected their own progress in nuclear weapons and delivery systems to neutralize American military power and divide the Western alliance, this expectation has proven unfounded. American military power remains a credible and effective deterrent to aggressive Soviet policies. This was abundantly clear in the Cuban crisis of 1962, which I believe was resolved as it was because the Russians were under no illusions about the over-all strategic superiority of the United States. Two basic points were demonstrated to the Soviet government by the Cuban crisis: that their own nuclear power did not neutralize that of the United States and that any attempt on their part to overturn the existing balance of military power would involve unacceptable risks.

The West, paradoxically, may find within a very few years that it is suffering from an embarrassment of power in its dealings with the Soviet Union. If, as seems probable, the strength of Western Europe continues to grow, the scales of world political, economic, and military power will become increasingly weighted on the side of the West, creating a situation in which Soviet apprehensions, especially as to Germany, will become greatly intensified. The dangers of such a situation are obvious. When a great power is confronted with an increasingly unfavorable disequilibrium in the scales of world power, it may be tempted, as I have suggested, to act rashly to reverse the trend.

Other than by very limited efforts to act directly on Soviet public opinion, I do not know precisely how the West can deal with this potential problem, which, if it develops, will be a product of the success of the West in shaping a powerful and coherent partnership. I do feel very certain, however, that Western statesmen should be thinking hard and long about the possible consequences of a major shift in the balance of power. Clearly, it is not in our interests to divest ourselves of strength, which is essential to our own security and to our long-term hopes for a safer, more rational world order. At the same time we must not delude ourselves into supposing that the Soviet Union is a nation which can be expected to float becalmed on a tide of unfavorable events. It would be a profoundly ironic tragedy if the growing strength and unity of the West, instead of providing it with security and peace, were instead to provoke an act of desperation on the part of a powerful adversary who has become convinced that he must either strike or go under.

We must not confront the Russians with this draconic choice. We must act always on the principle that power represents the gravest kind of danger to those who possess it as well as to their adversaries unless it is exercised with responsibility and restraint, and that the greater the power, the greater the need for responsibility in its use.

In this connection, I think that there is a lesson for us in the way that Britain exercised her pre-eminent power in the nineteenth century. The foundation of the *Pax Britannica* was not solely the preponderance of British naval and economic power but the great restraint with which it was exercised. When the Napoleonic wars ended in 1815, Britain was in possession of nearly all of the overseas colonies of France and the other continental powers and was certainly in a position to retain them. She chose, however, to return most of them for the very sensible reason that she did not wish to provoke a continental alignment against herself as the sole possessor of colonies. For the sake of her own security, Britain restored the French colonies as hostages to British sea power. Throughout the nineteenth century Britain preserved her power by so exercising it that, for the most part, it did not threaten the vital interests of the continental powers and, therefore, did not provoke them into forming a coalition which might have destroyed it.

The analogy, of course, is far from perfect, but the lesson is clear. As I have said, I am not certain as to precisely how this lesson should be applied under present and potential circumstances. I am, however, very certain that the failure to apply it could have catastrophic consequences.

·　　·　　·

THE PROPOSITION that the United States and its allies should under certain circumstances deliberately refrain from exercising the fullest measure of their power against a dangerous and aggressive adversary is not one which readily commends itself to many Americans, including some who hold high elective office. We are told by such persons that

31

the goal of our foreign policy should be "total victory" over Communism, or at any rate that we should *declare* our goal to be "total victory."

I am not at all sure what "total victory" means, although there is no doubt that the term has an exhilarating ring, nor do I find myself greatly enlightened by the explanation which has been offered that "victory is the opposite of defeat." The difficulty here arises from a confusion of ends and means. "Victory," like "unconditional surrender," is not a goal but rather one possible condition for the achievement of goals. As we learned after World War II, the "unconditional surrender" of our enemies, far from representing the realization of a new and better world order, instead represented a condition, a negative condition that contributed to subsequent developments which were far from pleasing to the Western democracies. It seems appropriate, therefore, to raise two questions about the concept of "total victory" as an objective of national policy.

The first of these questions is how such a victory is to be won. Is it to be won by some brilliant stroke of diplomacy which has thus far eluded us, by rational arguments of such devastating logic that the Communists will be persuaded to abandon their expansionist policies? Or is "total victory" to be won by a nuclear war which at the very least would cost the lives of tens of millions of people on both sides, devastate most or all of our great cities, and mutilate or utterly destroy our civilization?

Even more perplexing than the question of winning "total victory" is the second question, which is: what would we do with it once it were won? That is to say, how would we utilize the condition of victory in order to realize a desirable or important goal of policy? The precedents of past "total victories," such as that of our Civil War and the reconstruction era which followed, are hardly encouraging. Even assuming that we could somehow manage the immense technical problems of occupying the vast territories of our defeated enemies and finding the human and material resources with which to "re-educate" hundreds of millions of people, are we really certain that we have the incalculable qualitative resources of wisdom, vision, and compassion with which to reconstruct the world according to the specifications of absolute morality? To answer this question in the affirmative would require a degree of moral and intellectual arrogance that would do credit to the most fanatical and unreconstructed Marxian idealogue.

If there is any absolutely reliable lesson that we can derive from the history of nations, it is that there are limitations to policy, profound limitations which reflect the imperfections of human nature and which cannot be overcome by noble designs and grandiose declarations. The mature nation, like the mature man, is one which has made a workable accommodation between its aspirations and its limitations. We are neither omniscient nor omnipotent and, however much we might wish to do so, we cannot aspire to make the world over in our image.

Two "total victories" won by the West in the two total wars of the twentieth century have generated many more problems than they have solved. The price of these victories was the loss of the world-wide hegemony of the Western nations. The price of a third such "total victory" would be the probable destruction of Western civilization as we know it. As Walter Lippmann has pointed out, a nuclear war

33

would not be followed by a Marshall Plan or any other form of reconstruction but by a savage struggle for survival by the wretched survivors. A nuclear war would produce the greatest convulsion in history, resulting, at the very least, in the destruction of our American freedoms and institutions.[15]

On November 29, 1917, the *Daily Telegraph* of London published a letter by Lord Lansdowne about the damage to be wrought by the war then in progress. His prophecy, which was scornfully rejected at the time but tragically vindicated in the outcome, is even more compelling for our own time. "We are going to win the war," he wrote, ". . . but its prolongation will spell the ruin of the civilized world, and an infinite addition to the load of human suffering which already weighs upon it. Security will be invaluable to a world which has the vitality to profit by it, but what will be the value of the blessings of peace to nations so exhausted that they can scarcely stretch out a hand with which to grasp them?"[16]

It is clear beyond doubt that modern war—especially a nuclear war but also the two world wars already fought to "total victory"—entails evils that outweigh any possible benefits of victory. It is no longer possible, if ever it was, for the West to win by force a universal and unqualified victory for its ideas and values. An opportunity to win such a victory came to us for a brief moment in history in the year 1919, when the Western democracies were predominant in the world with no totalitarian adversaries strong enough to resist their will. Woodrow Wilson perceived this unexampled opportunity and strove mightily to realize its promise, but the failure of the succeeding generation was swift and com-

34

plete. The men who came after Wilson were neither great nor wise, but even if they had been, the promise of a universal moral order might have been lost because of the sheer grandeur of its conception, and because men are simply not capable of such great things all at once and on so grand a scale. My own conviction is that it would have been far better for the world if statesmen had succeeded in 1914 in patching up the defective old order of things, which, however imperfect, was not uncivilized by twentieth-century standards and which, if carefully husbanded by sensible and practical men, might well have evolved toward the promise of a safe and rational world order which now seems so hopelessly beyond our reach.

There is little to be gained in our efforts to solve the problems of the present by nostalgic regrets about the lost hopes of the past, but there is a great deal to be gained by examining how and why these hopes were lost. They were lost, I think, because we exceeded the bounds of human limitations and, aspiring to too much, failed of lesser goals which, through more modest efforts, we might have gained.

As applied to the Western response to the Soviet challenge in the years to come, the burden of these considerations is clear. It is that there are many options open to us besides the extremes of "total victory" and defeat. It is within our power, if we are wise and strong and patient, to shape our own destiny toward the fulfillment of the highest values of our civilization while encouraging the forces of moderation and common sense that are by no means entirely absent from Soviet society. We can do these things by using all of the instruments of policy—political and military, economic and cultural—to make the West so strong that rational leaders of the Soviet Union will be permanently confronted with a situation in which the Marxist-Leninist vision of world dominion is a dangerous and unattainable dream. At the same time we can make it clear to the Soviets that they have nothing to fear from the West, that they can have a secure and untroubled national existence under institutions of their choice, which, though repugnant to the West, will never of themselves be the occasion or cause of conflict.

The issue between the Soviet Union and the West is not "Communism versus capitalism," but the universal and unlimited aims of Soviet policy. In the words of the French journalist and scholar Raymond Aron: "Should the Soviets ever recognize that their regime is only one of a number of possible ways of organizing industrial societies, the majority of democrats—while continuing to regard certain practices of the Soviet regime as deplorable, inefficient or inhuman—would no longer feel obliged to maintain an attitude of active hostility to the Soviet Union."[17]

The real issue between the two conflicting civilizations will not be decided at the frontiers where they confront each other or by the direct action of one upon the other, but by what happens within each of the two societies. In this respect the distinction between foreign and domestic policy evaporates, because the ultimate decision between two competing systems of economic and political organization will be determined by which is more successful in meeting the material and spiritual needs of man. If the issue is ultimately resolved in favor of the democratic values of the West, it will be because we, more successfully than our adversaries, have created an economic system that provides material abundance, a political system based on justice and freedom

36

and human dignity, and an educational system that culti-
vates individual excellence and spiritual fulfillment.

If we do these things, always remembering that man's
capacity to do good things, though great, is not unlimited,
then we may arrive before too long at a time in history
which, in Woodrow Wilson's words, is "not perhaps a
golden age, but at any rate an age which is brightening from
decade to decade and may lead us some time to an elevation
from which we can see the things for which the heart of
mankind has longed."[18]

# 2 · A CONCERT OF FREE NATIONS

"THE NATIONS seem to be advancing to unity," wrote Alexis de Tocqueville in 1835. "Our means of intellectual intercourse unite the most remote parts of the earth; and it is impossible for men to remain strangers to each other, or to be ignorant of the events which are taking place in any corner of the globe."[1]

Perceiving the possibility of world community, Tocqueville took it for probability; he failed to take account of the human capacity for contact without communication, for knowledge without understanding. Far from leading to a community of mankind, the economic and technological unification of the world has in fact aggravated, and made far more dangerous, the animosities of national communities that continue to value their separate sovereignty over their common humanity and even their security. Only in the lands bordering the North Atlantic has a tendency toward community recently taken hold, and even here the trend has been fragmentary, hesitant, and of uncertain duration.

For at least a century and a half Western history has been shaped by two great contradictory forces, one a tendency toward cooperation and community, the other a baleful nationalism that set the nations against each other and culminated in the great conflicts of the twentieth century. In our own time there is reason to hope that the great paradox is at last moving toward resolution in favor of a broad community of the North Atlantic peoples. Great obstacles remain to be overcome, however, and as we have had occasion to note in recent history, no trend is irreversible. As of 1963 the unity of the West is neither certain nor even probable; it is no more than a reasonably well-founded hope.

The tendency toward community in the Western world developed in the wake of the Napoleonic wars. The victors of that conflict, more interested in future peace than past grievances, granted generous terms to the vanquished and devised a rudimentary council of great powers vested with the responsibility for preserving peace and stability in Europe. Out of the Vienna settlement of 1815 grew the Concert of Europe, a rough-hewn but genuine community of nations which valued their common interest in preserving peace and the balance of power over their conflicting national aspirations. The Concert of Europe represented a limited, indeed a primitive, community and it enforced a fragile system of law, but it kept the peace for a hundred years—a most impressive achievement by twentieth-century standards. The collapse of the concert and the end of the long peace were the result of both fortuitous events and deeply rooted forces. Among these forces the most important by far was the rise of aggressive nationalism.

The national unification and independence movements of the nineteenth century for a time contributed to the trend toward broader community. These movements in their early stages were closely associated with democratic and humanitarian ideas. As expressed in the writings of Bentham and Mill, Guizot and Mazzini, nineteenth-century nationalism was liberal and high-minded, peaceful and optimistic. In the final decades of the nineteenth century, the link be-

39

tween nationalist and liberal democratic ideas was severed
and nationalism became chauvinist, militarist, and aggressive. Under the impact of mounting national rivalries the
old Concert of Europe became progressively enfeebled until
it was finally shattered by the explosion of unbridled
nationalism.

The great paradox was the simultaneous growth of the
force for unity and the force for division. To the eternal
detriment of the West and the world it was the divisive force
that prevailed. The collapse in 1914 of an imperfect but not
uncivilized old order was precipitated by unforeseen accidents and uncontrolled events. Though perhaps not inevitable, these events were made possible by the disintegration
of the international community of shared values which had
given Europe a century of relative peace. Thus it occurred
that Europe and the world were drawn into a vortex of
conflict that statesmen who had neither planned nor desired
it were powerless to prevent.

It is not necessary to rehearse the tragic events of the
era of two world wars that all but destroyed Europe. Lasting
from 1914 until 1945, the "civil war" of the West took tens
of millions of lives, wrought incalculable material and moral
damage, destroyed the world-wide hegemony of Western
ideas and interests and institutions, and left the West beset
by graver threats and a more formidable antagonist than it
had ever before confronted. Such were the rewards of
unbridled nationalism.

In the last half-century the "European age" has come to
a close. The passing of European pre-eminence in the world
and the emergence of a global system controlled by two non-
European powers of continental size mean something more

than an alteration of power relationships. As one contemporary writer has put it: "What is meant is that a particular form of political organization, based upon the nation-state, is no longer the determining pattern in world affairs. For European history since at least the close of the Middle Ages has been the history of conflicting and competing nation-states, as Mediterranean history was the record of rival city-states. To say that the European age has closed is to imply that the nation-state is no longer the dominant political form."[2]

The end of the "European age" was brought on by the expansion of the nation-state system beyond Europe itself, westward to include America and eastward to include Russia. As "peripheral" powers, America and Russia were beyond the control of the balance-of-power system which prevented any European nation from becoming significantly larger or more powerful than any other. The non-European nations were permitted to grow to continental dimensions and to develop power commensurate with their size while Europe remained divided against itself, seeking a tenuous stability at the cost of fragmentation. In the two world wars of the twentieth century Europe proved unable to resolve its internal conflicts by its own efforts, and the outcome of both conflicts was determined by the intervention of the non-European powers. America and Russia became the arbiters of a global political system of which Europe could never again be the single source and center.

.     .     .

WHAT IS to replace the classical "European age" is the central question confronting the Western world. On this question depends our own internal evolution, our future relations with the Communist world, and the character of our future bonds with Asia, Africa, and Latin America. One alternative, that of General de Gaulle, is to revive the old system on a global scale, to bring a confederated Europe under French hegemony into a world system that would be governed by the same rules as those which governed Europe in its era of pre-eminence. The other possibility, that of Atlantic partnership, is to alter the game as well as its players, to move beyond the system of a precarious equilibrium of sovereign entities toward a partnership encompassing all the Western people who share the experience of industrialism and political democracy.

The conflict between the Gaullist and Atlantic approaches is not a matter of mere misunderstanding, failure of communication, or personal predilection. The fundamental issue is one between two different conceptions of the future organization of the West and the world. The Gaullist design, it seems to me, is bold and even creative in tactics but profoundly conservative in its objectives. It seeks to reshape Europe as an essentially *national* entity which would be large enough and strong enough to participate as a great power in a world-wide system of nation-states related to each other in the traditional patterns of rivalry and balance. The Gaullist program is designed to restore and conserve the classical balance-of-power system among sovereign nations, with its inherent instability, by adjusting it to the specifications of the age of super-states and nuclear weapons.

The Atlantic conception, on the other hand, is built on the premise that an international system based on unlimited national sovereignty has become an intolerably dangerous

42

anachronism in the nuclear age, not only for small nations but for great nations as well—indeed especially for great nations. Like the League of Nations Covenant and the United Nations Charter, the idea of Atlantic partnership is an attempt to come to grips with the basic facts of world politics in the twentieth century: that modern warfare has become so destructive that it has ceased to be a rational instrument of national policy; that the international system that worked tolerably well to prevent or limit war before 1914 has broken down irreparably in the last half-century; and that if we are to survive under these new conditions the nation-state can no longer serve as the ultimate unit of law and human association.

The collapse of the League of Nations and the failure of the United Nations thus far to achieve the hopes that attended its creation were not the result of their repudiation of an old order which had failed, but rather the result of an effort to outrun history, to move in a single leap from world anarchy to world community. Unfortunately there is no necessary correlation between human need and human capacity. However fully it may comport with our needs, the shaping of a genuine world community is demonstrably beyond our capacity in the world as it is and as it is likely to be for the foreseeable future. We must therefore focus our efforts on the more modest goal of building new bonds among those peoples of the free world who have some feeling of shared values and interests, some feeling of the ability to communicate effectively, some feeling of trust and confidence in each other's purposes.

These feelings are the preconditions of community. They exist, I believe, in substantial measure among the industrial

43

democracies of the North Atlantic area. Because they do, Atlantic partnership is a feasible goal, barely feasible perhaps, but nonetheless one which we can pursue with some reasonably well-founded hope of success. If it is far short of the universal aims of the United Nations Charter, it is also far bolder and more creative than the Gaullist vision of a unified but exclusive Europe. The Atlantic idea, in short, represents the point at which our needs and our capacity seem to converge.

The minimum price of survival in this century will be our continuing effort to forge new and deeper bonds of cooperation among nations and, beyond this, to begin to divert some part of our feelings of loyalty and responsibility from the sovereign nation to a broader association of peoples. Among the myths and misconceptions that have brought the West to disaster, the most destructive and pervasive of our time has been the idea of the nation as a kind of spiritual entity with a will and a sanctity of its own transcending the individuals who compose it. Far from being the spiritual organism of nationalist mythology, the modern nation-state is the product of the historical evolution of human groups from their tribal origins to ever larger forms of social organization, not as the result of some mystical force of history, but in response to very practical economic, military, and political needs. In the twentieth century the mythology of the sovereign nation delimits the bonds among men, confining those bonds within political communities no longer capable of satisfying the requirements of security and economic growth. The concept of absolute national sovereignty is thus a principle of international anarchy. If the real needs of the West and of the world are to be met, we will have to alter in the most fundamental manner the traditional concepts of national sovereignty and self-determination.

The process of alteration is already well-advanced in the Europe of the Six. In the most rational and sensible way, the members of the European Economic Community have launched a successful revolution—a new kind of revolution that does not attempt to outrun history. The great success of the Common Market has derived from its working principle that new institutions must be built on the solid foundations of community and cohesion. "Just as language precedes grammar," said Walter Hallstein in his Clayton Lectures of 1961–62, "so politics precedes political theory; and disputes as to the proper terminology for what we are doing in the European Community sometimes seem to me as academic as grammarians' controversies."[3]

The European Community has applied what may be called "the Jean Monnet theory of change." Monnet uses the metaphor of a mountain path. From the bottom there is one view; from a point halfway up, another; from the top, quite another. A man standing at the bottom cannot possibly have the view of a man standing at the top, or halfway up. To change his view, you must get him to start moving up, however slowly. As soon as he has moved he will have a different view, perhaps a better one, and the improvement may induce him to take another step.[4] The question that now troubles and divides the West is whether Europe, having begun the ascent up the "mountain path," will continue toward the summit or abandon the ascent at the precarious plateau which has now been reached.

It would be a tragedy of incalculable proportions if the

great hopes and opportunities which the West now has were to be lost in the only possible way they could be lost, by the division of the West into separate and competing communities. Reluctantly but irrevocably, America in the last generation has abandoned its traditional isolation, recognizing that in this age of nuclear weapons and scientific revolution even so large and powerful a nation as the United States can be neither secure nor prosperous in isolation. Similarly, free Europe must recognize that even a united and thriving continent is too small a community to confront alone the dangers and opportunities of our time. Europe must not repeat the pattern of the national unification movements of a century ago, which at first broadened but then confined the frontiers of European community and thus culminated in the magnified national rivalries that destroyed the Concert of Europe. A new "European" nationalism, or a renewed American isolationism, would represent the abandonment of our ascent up the mountain and the defeat of our highest hopes.

It is sometimes suggested that a united Europe could act as a "third force," a mediator between the United States and the Soviet Union. This idea, in my opinion, is irresponsible nonsense. It rests on the faulty premise that the world struggle between Communism and freedom is essentially a Soviet-American conflict, in which other countries are at liberty to participate or not as it suits their interests and convenience. There is in fact no such option open to any of the Atlantic nations unless one accepts the irrational proposition that it is possible to be neutral between one's friends and one's enemies. Communist imperialism is a common danger to the entire Atlantic community and the

46

entire free world, a danger that has been imposed upon all of us in equal and impartial measure. Because this is true, it is no more possible for Europe to be "neutral" than for America to return to isolation.

The current crisis in the Western alliance is not a petty quarrel over prestige or personalities. It is a debate on the fundamental question of how the Western community is to be organized now that Europe's postwar dependency on the United States is at an end. The demand of a resurgent Europe for a status in the world commensurate with its new strength is a natural historical development which is based on much more permanent foundations than the personality and ambitions of General de Gaulle. It is General de Gaulle, however, who is currently giving voice and content to Europe's self-assertion and he is doing so in a manner which, in my opinion, is detrimental to the best interests of both Europe and America. Like Bismarck a hundred years ago, he pursues, with formidable skill and resourcefulness, a limited and inadequate vision of unification. His vision, like Bismarck's, would, if realized, unite a small community at the cost of dividing a larger one; it would sow the seeds of unnecessary and unnatural animosities among peoples whose destinies, like their histories, are inextricably bound together.

If we are to cope with the Gaullist challenge, we must begin by recognizing the true sources of its power. The "new reality," as Walter Lippmann has defined it, is that Western Europe has outgrown the dependence upon America which began with the First World War and will no longer accept American pre-eminence in European affairs. The "new reality" is the result of the great changes of the last decade: the brilliant recovery of Western Europe, the decline of the United States from world financial preeminence, the failure of the United States to cope with chronic economic sluggishness, and the shifting of the military balance of power in favor of the West with the result that the Soviet military threat in Europe has greatly abated. The effect of these changes is that "Western Europe is much less dependent on the United States than it has been for nearly fifty years."[5]

Being "less dependent" is quite a different matter from being independent. Europe has become less dependent on the United States in the sense that the threat of imminent catastrophe—of war and of political and economic collapse —has receded after a generation of turmoil. In terms of continuing interests, on the other hand, of long-term security and stability, of the opportunity to realize our full economic potential and to improve the lives of our people, Europe and America remain profoundly dependent upon each other. In close partnership Western Europe and America have it within their power to attain greater security than they have known in this century, to help the underdeveloped countries to overcome their ancient affliction of poverty, to bring unexampled material well-being to their own people and, in so doing, to liberate them for the creative pursuits of civilized society.

The postwar era is past. If we are to adjust to this fact and to realize the opportunities of Atlantic unity, we must reconsider the major components of our foreign policy. Fortunately the current crisis in the Western alliance does not pose an immediate threat to our security and we have time in which to think about the new circumstances which confront us and how best to deal with them. General de Gaulle has struck a blow at the foundations of postwar American policy. The General's challenge has been carefully conceived and skillfully executed and it is not going to be overcome by precipitate action or by spiteful acts of retaliation. My own view is that there are certain specific steps which we can take toward restoring Western unity but that there is little we can do for the present that would strike at the heart of the problem.

Because the dangers posed by Western disunity are long-range rather than immediate, we would do well to reflect for a time on where we stand and where we are going before making major new policy decisions. Specifically, we must think about four main areas of relations among the Western countries: their defense, their trade, their political and institutional bonds with one another, and their common responsibilities toward the less developed nations. In each of these areas there may be limited measures which can be taken in the immediate future. In none of them does the time seem ripe for major new policy departures.

.      .      .

THE MEANING of the current debate in the Atlantic Alliance on the control of nuclear weapons was recently explained by Lord Crathorne in these words: "The Atlantic provides the essential depth of security for our perilous strip of freedom in Western Europe, and not its boundary. This, for the first time since the beginning of the Alliance, . . . is being thrown to question. A new and alternative reading of history, and indeed of geography, is being suggested—namely, that the North Atlantic represents three

49

thousand miles of water separating two essentially different segments in the Western world, each of which must work out its separate salvation."[6]

I do not know how the problem of Western defense, and particularly of the control of nuclear weapons, is going to be resolved. Nor do I feel qualified to offer a formula for its resolution. I feel certain, however, that no arrangement will provide real or lasting security unless it is built on the principle of the indivisibility of Western defense. Until a few years ago it was the United States which felt its safety was unrelated to the safety of Western Europe. Having been drawn against its will into the two great European wars of the twentieth century, the United States has abandoned the untenable theory of isolationism and now, in a curious reversal of roles, it is Europe which is tempted by illusions of neutrality. "One striking irony of the cold war," writes Robert Osgood, "is that now the formerly isolationist United States, by virtue of her preponderant power, feels more directly involved in the practical tasks of the power conflict than her front-line allies, who are tempted to view this conflict with something of the disdain, aloofness, and escapism with which Americans once viewed the Old World. Yet the security of the European allies is far more directly and immediately involved in the toils of NATO than the security of the United States was ever involved in the toils of European politics during the heyday of American isolation."[7]

Our European allies are quite properly demanding a measure of authority in the direction of the Alliance commensurate with their new strength and weight. At the same time they have shown little enthusiasm for taking on greater responsibilities in conventional arms and in other important areas such as foreign aid where the United States continues to carry a disproportionate burden. This problem has become acute because of the American balance-of-payments problem and because of the relative sluggishness of the American economy compared to that of Europe.

Adequate conventional as well as nuclear power is essential to provide the West with a wide range of options other than nuclear holocaust. Such balanced strength is necessary for a strategy of controlled response to whatever provocations confront us. In no way does it imply a retreat by the United States from its commitment to use its nuclear strike force in the defense of Europe. Our commitment to the defense of Europe is absolute and irrevocable—so long as the critical decisions that lead to war or peace are not removed beyond our influence and responsibility. What a strategy of controlled response does imply is that the security of the West cannot depend solely, even though it depends primarily, on our nuclear deterrent. Indeed, the very credibility of our deterrent power depends upon our ability to deter lesser as well as greater provocations. As President Kennedy has said, we must have "a wider choice than humiliation or all-out nuclear action." To this end, we need both nuclear superiority and non-nuclear options.

The two basic problems of Western defense, building a stronger conventional system and devising a workable method of joint control of the nuclear deterrent, must be solved together. Anxieties over the control of strategic nuclear weapons are exacerbated by the excessive dependence on these weapons which is caused by an inadequate capacity to repel conventional aggression by conventional means. Europe, it seems clear, is capable of a greater contribution to NATO's conventional forces. The United States in turn must be receptive to Europe's legitimate desire for greater participation in the control of nuclear weapons. Tangible progress toward the achievement of consensus on a strategy of controlled and graduated response, supported by the required conventional forces, would greatly facilitate the problems of nuclear control.

There is no ready solution to the problem of joint command decision in the use of nuclear weapons. Responsibility is inseparable from power, and wars, certainly nuclear war, cannot be conducted by committees. As long as the United States controls the vast preponderance of Western nuclear power, it is bound to retain ultimate responsibility for their use or non-use. The creation of a multilateral seaborne nuclear force will go a way toward meeting Europe's demand for nuclear sharing, but it is only a palliative, albeit a costly one, that does not go to the heart of the problem. The vast land-based and airborne nuclear capacity of the United States will continue under sole American control and, with it, the ultimate authority to decide on war or peace. It seems to me, therefore, that the creation of a multilateral nuclear force, though a desirable exercise in NATO cooperation, will not solve the problem of giving Europe an adequate voice in determining the conditions of its own survival.

Even more unpromising are proposals for a separate and independent European nuclear force, the so-called "dumbbell" approach. In the first place, it may well be questioned whether our European allies would be likely to trust each other's decisions on war and peace any more than they trust American judgment. But even if such a force could be brought into operating existence, it would do little more than duplicate the existing Western deterrent at enormous expense. Furthermore it would be more likely to act as a trigger to involve the United States than to relieve us of our responsibilities for the defense of Europe. It is inconceivable that either Europe or America could remain neutral if the other were attacked, or that the Soviet Union would allow either to stand aside. There can be nothing but danger, therefore, in a divided Western defense. It would expose both Europe and America to the constant possibility of being drawn into war without their own consent. The existence of this possibility would itself generate mutual fear and distrust within the Western Alliance, posing the danger of deep and lasting divisions in every dimension of our relations.

The worst possible outcome of the current debate, of course, would be the multiplication of separate national nuclear arsenals. In addition to being prohibitively expensive and of dubious strategic value, the proliferation of national nuclear arsenals would undermine the foundation of Western political and military collaboration and inject a powerful new element of instability into the world balance of power.

A unified Western strategy is thus essential to our future peace and security. We must find a way to bring our allies into meaningful participation in the vital decisions relating to war and peace. The crux of the problem is the development of a solid strategic consensus among the NATO allies. The development of such a consensus can be approached through a system of allied participation in the planning and shaping of strategic policy, in determining the *condi-*

*tions* under which the American deterrent would be brought to bear. This, if successful, would provide a basis for ultimate allied control of the nuclear deterrent itself. Once full consensus were achieved, it is unlikely that technical and organizational problems would prove to be insurmountable. In the final analysis, the control of missiles and warheads is secondary to the control of basic policy processes that determine war or peace.

A unified system of strategic planning would serve many purposes. It would in the first place give Europe the voice in determining its own destiny that it rightly demands. More important perhaps in the long run, by elevating the debate on strategic policy from the domestic level to the level of the Alliance as a whole, it would generate an attitude toward Western defense as the defense of a single community. One can conceive of a unified strategic planning system helping to solve immediate problems and at the same time contributing to the broader purposes of Atlantic community.

There are impressive examples of joint planning and policy formation in specific functional areas in the wartime experience of Western nations—examples that may have some bearing on the current problems of the Western Alliance.

During the First World War the Allied and Associated Powers dealt through international agencies with such problems as the coordination of military strategy, the allocation of shipping, and the maintenance of supplies of food and raw materials. The Supreme War Council under Marshal Foch became virtually an international cabinet for the conduct of the war. Before the war was over, some

European statesmen began to think of it as a "rudimentary league of nations." A number of other functional international organs operated with great success during the war and the Peace Conference.

Even more impressive achievements of close coordination, indeed unification, of policy were achieved by Great Britain and the United States in World War II. The grand strategy of the war was shaped through intimate consultations between President Roosevelt and Prime Minister Churchill, and the British and American armed forces were put under a joint command, the Combined Chiefs of Staff. Under the direction of the political leaders of the two countries, the Combined Chiefs of Staff, sitting in Washington, formulated and executed policies and plans relating to the strategic conduct of the war, allocation of munitions, and transportation requirements. A close working relationship developed between the top British representative, Field Marshal Sir John Dill, and General George Marshall, who together made policy decisions in an informal manner. The Allied war effort was also unified by a system of combined boards whose task was to muster the full economic resources of Great Britain and the United States and Canada.

The experience of the joint war effort points to the efficacy of a functional approach toward the building of an international community. In the performance of critically important but clearly limited tasks the Allies tended not so much to reject as to forget their separate nationality. A sense of community arose from practical association in a common enterprise. In the words of a writer who has made a comprehensive study of Allied cooperation in World War II: "The larger conclusion to be drawn from the experience of the war lies perhaps in the fact that under great stress men were capable of organized effort commensurate with the magnitude of the task with which they were confronted. In the emergency they contributed to the commonweal far beyond their usual efforts. They developed loyalties toward higher goals and the larger group, which ordinary times do not readily foster. In many instances they experienced for the first time the full meaning of social responsibility. Similarly, they met the crisis through organizational innovation and ingenuity."[8]

In times of clear and present danger, custom, inertia, vested interests, and traditional viewpoints give way to the demands of the times. The problem that now confronts NATO is whether it can meet the requirements of a long-term rather than an immediate danger with a spirit similar to that which motivated the Western Allies in the two world wars. If we can forge something like the unity of purpose and common action that we so successfully forged in wartime, we will be well on the way toward a solution of the problem of nuclear weapons control as well as toward meeting the broader challenge of building an Atlantic community.

A unified strategic planning system along the lines of the arrangements worked out in the two world wars can be devised within the existing framework of NATO. This requires both reforms in the policy machinery of NATO and, what is more important, a new attitude of trust and confidence among the present allies. No alliance can long survive if each member bases its policies on the assumption that its partners will honor their commitments only so long as they find it easy and convenient to do so. It is true that there have been instances of poor judgment and insensitivity in relations within the Alliance, notably on the part of Britain and the United States, which have a way at times of forgetting that there are other countries in the Alliance. It is imperative, therefore, that the English-speaking countries overcome some of the pretensions and limitations of their "special relationship." At the same time some of our European partners might improve their own perspective by adopting an attitude toward the occasional lapses of the "Anglo-Saxons" something like that of an Austrian Ambassador in London of fifty years ago, who counseled his government that "A good deal that we interpret as deceit is in fact merely the result of ignorance and superficiality, and is due to carelessness and confusion."[9]

There is little need of new machinery for unified strategic planning and policy coordination in the Western Alliance. Existing NATO machinery can adequately serve these purposes with certain reforms and, above all, with a concerted will to use this machinery effectively. There is no reason, for example, why the NATO Council cannot in time be developed into a strategic planning body on the model of the Combined Chiefs of Staff of World War II. What is needed in the Western Alliance is not elaborate new machinery, which could all too easily be left to atrophy, but the invigoration of existing NATO organs by the application of a strong new spirit of partnership and trust.

The most useful single step toward the strengthening of NATO as a meaningful instrument of Atlantic partnership would be the elevation of the NATO Council to the stature of a genuine organ of policy coordination. As things now stand the Council is neither equipped nor authorized

57

to serve this purpose. It lacks, for example, an adequate secretariat to carry out the tasks of long-range policy planning. In addition, the Council lacks effective authority over military planning in the Standing Group and Supreme Allied Headquarters in Europe, with the result that political consultations and military planning are divided into separate compartments.

One major way of enhancing the status of the NATO Council would be to assign to it men of great political standing in their respective countries, men who could consult directly with and report directly to their heads of government. Such a step would considerably increase the authority of the Council's views and recommendations. The author of this proposal, Alastair Buchan, the Director of the Institute for Strategic Studies in London, explains its necessity in these words: "If the inherent disadvantages of a large alliance when confronting a single adversary are to be overcome, it is as important in times of tension to have a political operations center as a military one; in an alliance of democracies this can be manned only by men who wield political authority in their own countries."[10]

One can readily conceive of an enhanced NATO Council as the organ of consultation in the shaping of Western nuclear strategy. It could become the forum for long-term political and military planning on the most fundamental questions of war and peace. Through the gradual formulation of an over-all strategic consensus among the Atlantic allies, a strengthened NATO Council could in time resolve the problems of nuclear sharing that now seem insuperable.

It is quite possible that such a major enhancement of the NATO policy machinery would not at first commend itself to all of our partners. Should this still be the case after a considerable period of debate and discussion, it would be appropriate, I think, to proceed with those of our allies who are prepared to cooperate, leaving an "empty chair" and a standing invitation for the reluctant or laggard. The affairs of the Alliance are far too important to be governed indefinitely by the veto of its least cooperative member. The strengthening of NATO, and particularly of the NATO Council, is one of the advances toward full Atlantic partnership that can and should be undertaken without excessive delay. Such measures are both strategically necessary and politically feasible. They are in line not only with our needs but also with the feasibilities of history.

.    .    .

NO LESS important than the question of nuclear weapons and defense for the Alliance is the challenge of shaping new economic relations among the Atlantic countries. The kind of economic community envisaged by the Treaty of Rome and by the American Trade Expansion Act of 1962 has vast political as well as economic implications. As one contemporary writer has commented: "The reduction of tariff barriers and all the other economic changes which the treaties have set in motion are the outward signs of integration, but at its center lies a profound shift in political relationships, political methods, and political objectives."[11]

The Trade Expansion Act was the American response to the liberal spirit of Article 110 of the Treaty of Rome, which set forth the intention of the European Community "to contribute, in conformity with the common interest, to the harmonious development of world trade, the progressive abolition of restrictions on international exchanges, and the lowering of customs barriers." The new American approach on trade, adopted in the wake of a significant campaign of national persuasion and education, will fulfill its promise only if the European Community keeps faith with the spirit and intent of Article 110 of the Treaty of Rome. The progressive lowering of tariff barriers, despite transitory hardships and adjustments on both sides, would open the way to substantially expanded trade and accelerated economic growth for both Europe and America. Beyond this, the development of a thriving economic community of the North Atlantic would have enormous implications, political as well as economic, for the entire free world. In the words of a recent Senate Foreign Relations Committee staff study: "From the spreading base of this mutually beneficial trade, the two great communities on either side of the Atlantic should be able to perform a number of tasks that have become indivisible, to reach major goals that neither could reach alone."[12]

An Atlantic trading partnership is neither a conception of pure idealism nor, as certain Europeans have suggested, a sublimated form of American economic colonialism. It is a conception based on the realities of mutual advantage, a project rooted in solid foundations of interest for both Europe and America. The United States needs to participate in a large Atlantic trading area in order to expand its trade and thus be able to earn the hard money needed to finance its military and civilian commitments overseas. If the European Economic Community becomes a closed, restrictive trading area, the United States will be unable to earn the costs of financing its contribution to the defense of

Europe. With our mounting obligations in Latin America and Asia and a substantial annual deficit in our balance of payments, we would eventually have no choice but to reduce our contribution to Western European defense. An Atlantic trading partnership is thus far more than a noble dream; it is a necessity of the first priority for both Europe and America.

For these reasons, General de Gaulle's apparent design for a restrictive, protectionist European economy, at least in the area of agriculture, poses the greatest possible threat to the real interests of France's partners in the Common Market as well as those of America, and indeed of France herself. In his press conference of January 14, 1963, General de Gaulle left no doubt about his ideas for an autarchic European agricultural economy. "The system of the Six," he said, "consists of making a pool of the agricultural products of the entire Community, of strictly determining their prices, of forbidding subsidizing, of organizing their consumption between all the members, and of making it obligatory for each of these members to pay the Community any savings they might make by having food stuffs brought in from outside instead of consuming those offered by the Common Market."

This means of course that the European consumer is to be denied access to the low-cost food products of the United States and other efficient producers and to be compelled to pay a heavy subsidy for the sustenance of French agriculture. Through the workings of the variable levy system, such low-cost American foodstuffs as wheat, poultry, and feed grains are to be excluded from the European market, creating a monopoly for relatively inefficient European producers at arbitrarily high prices. The German duty on poultry, for example, was raised in August 1962 from about $4\frac{1}{2}$ cents a pound to about 13 cents a pound, which, as Walter Lippmann commented, "is high enough to come near making isolationists out of the Senators from Arkansas and Georgia."[13] Since then it has been raised again to over 14 cents a pound.

A highly protectionist European agricultural policy would do immense damage to the foreign trade of the United States and other agricultural producers. If the Common Market maintains high tariffs against overseas farm products, the United States, according to a report prepared for the Joint Economic Committee of Congress, stands to lose as much as 30 percent of all its exports to Europe. The report predicts that the United States would lose most of the European market for wheat and poultry among other products.[14]

Foodstuffs account for approximately one third of all American exports to Europe. Should much or all of the European market be lost, our favorable balance of trade would turn into a deficit and our balance-of-payments problem would be gravely aggravated. In such an eventuality, it is difficult to see how we could avoid drastic action to protect the stability of the dollar.

The implications of European protectionism and autarchy are of course for more than commercial. I believe that the thrust and design of economic exclusiveness, as conceived by General de Gaulle, are toward the creation of a closed European political confederation under French control with German support. The inherent instability of such a European order is quite obvious, not least because of the improbability that a dynamic and productive Germany would long consent to the role of lieutenant in a French-dominated political system. But even if a closed Europe could be made politically viable, I believe, for reasons I have stated, that such a system would be inimical to the real interests of Europe (including France), of America, and of the entire free world.

The frontiers of freedom are wider than the frontiers of Europe. If a unified Europe is to make a lasting contribution to the security and prosperity of the free world of which it is an integral part, it must be as part of a broader concert of free nations. The heart of Western civilization embraces the entire community of Atlantic democracies, and our future depends less on what we do in confrontation with the Communist world than on the kind of relations we develop and the kind of society we build within our own world. Most especially, our future depends on whether we allow the West to succumb once again to divisive and destructive nationalism or whether we make it so strong and unified that no one will dare attack us and so prosperous and progressive that it will serve as a model and a magnet for the entire world—for the struggling nations of Asia and Africa, for the unhappy peoples of Eastern Europe, and ultimately perhaps, for the Russians themselves.

.        .        .

SINCE THE exclusion of Great Britain from the European Economic Community, there seems little likelihood for the foreseeable future of a broadening of institutional bonds among the Western nations. The ascent up the "mountain

63

path," to return to Jean Monnet's metaphor, has been temporarily blocked by the Gaullist landslide. It is not possible from our present perspective to foresee the kind of relationship which Britain will ultimately have with Europe or the kind of relationship which we will have with both. These are problems which we must live with for a while. Fortunately there is no great urgency about solving them and we would do well to use the present hiatus for some hard and serious thought about the kind of Atlantic political institutions we would like to shape, if any, and the kinds of sacrifices we would be willing to make, if any, to achieve them.

My own view has been that the most promising road toward Atlantic community is not the "federal" but the "functional" road, that is, measured advances toward cooperation in specific and limited fields. The functional approach was represented by the Brussels negotiations for British entrance into the European Economic Community, and is for the present foreclosed. We would perhaps do well, therefore, to consider certain limited measures of Atlantic cooperation in areas that remain open to us, with a view to keeping the spirit of Atlantic community alive while we think about more significant advances in the future and await the opportunity to make them.

One avenue of progress, albeit limited progress, that remains open to us is that of improving Atlantic parliamentary institutions. In January 1962 the Atlantic Convention of NATO Nations, an unofficial group of distinguished Europeans and Americans, issued the "Declaration of Paris," in which they recommended the establishment of Atlantic executive and judicial organs and the development of the NATO Parliamentarians' Conference into a consultative "Atlantic Assembly." In November 1962 the NATO Parliamentarians' Conference commissioned a special subcommittee to study this proposal. I believe that the establishment of a consultative Atlantic Assembly in the near future would be a desirable and feasible measure for the strengthening of the Atlantic community. The establishment of such a body of parliamentarians would have a salutary effect in alleviating the current atmosphere of disunity and recrimination within the Alliance.

This Atlantic Assembly of parliamentarians should serve as a consultative organ for both NATO and the Organization for Economic Cooperation and Development (OECD). It should consult on the full scope of Atlantic relations, military and political, economic and cultural, and also on the relations of the North Atlantic countries with Asia, Africa, and Latin America.

The constitution of an Atlantic Assembly would of course have to be carefully considered, but one can envision a body authorized to submit recommendations to both NATO and the OECD, which in turn would be expected to reply to all proposals either in writing or by the appearance of authorized representatives before the parliamentary body or its subsidiary organs. In addition, the delegates to the Assembly might be empowered to express their confidence or lack of confidence in specific actions or decisions of the two executive bodies. To accommodate those countries which are members of OECD but not of NATO, procedures might be devised for separate consideration of OECD and NATO matters so that the neutrals would be able to abstain entirely from all questions of the military alliance.

It is possible, indeed probable, that the contributions of an Atlantic Assembly would for some time be more symbolic than substantive. In no sense could its creation be regarded as the "answer" to the basic problem of Western unity. Its value for the foreseeable future would be as an organ of counsel and consultation, a forum for the practice of community on the Atlantic level, and an institutional symbol of our interdependence.

.        .        .

THE NATIONS of the West, in the discharge of their common obligations to the underdeveloped countries of Asia, Africa, and Latin America, have a surpassing opportunity to strengthen their bonds with each other and to lay the foundations for a world-wide concert of free nations. They can accomplish these great results by bringing to bear in unity and common purpose only a small part of their vast resources.

It has been said, but it bears repeating, that the nations of Asia, Africa, and Latin America are caught up in a great historic revolution. The essence of this revolution is the demand for human dignity, material and moral, and for an approach to equality with the privileged community of the West. The challenge which this poses for the Atlantic nations is expressed in words that Alexis de Tocqueville wrote more than a hundred years ago: "The nations of our time cannot prevent the conditions of men from becoming equal; but it depends upon themselves whether the principle of equality is to lead them to servitude or freedom, to knowledge or barbarism, to prosperity or to wretchedness."[15]

I think it is important to be quite clear about the nature of Western interests in relation to the poor countries of the world. Whatever the extent of its humanitarian motivation

66

and effect, our material assistance to the less developed countries, far from being "nonpolitical" or essentially commercial or altruistic in character, has profound political implications. Foreign aid is one of a number of instruments of policy by which the West seeks to bolster its own security, by fostering a world environment in which our kind of society, and the values in which it is rooted, can survive and flourish. Indeed an adequate conception of Western aid is not one which divorces aid from political objectives but rather one which divorces it from crude and shortsighted, trivial and superficial objectives, by linking it firmly to our most vital *long-range* political goals.

Corollary to acknowledging the political purposes of foreign aid is a clear recognition of the fact that a meaningful and effective aid program, far from *avoiding* intervention in the affairs of a recipient, in fact constitutes intervention of a most profound character. Its purpose is nothing less than the reshaping of a society, of its internal life and, in less obvious ways, of its relations with the outside world. Indeed the determinant of our aid—of whether or not we extend it and whether or not a country will wish to have it—must be the kind of internal changes it can be expected to bring about and the effect which these changes will have on the interests of both the donor and the recipient. "The moral here," as one perceptive student of Latin American affairs has put it, "is that a great power such as the United States necessarily intervenes in the affairs of other countries, especially smaller ones, as much by what it does not do as by what it does. A policy of nonintervention, if that term is interpreted in the strictest, most literal sense, becomes plainly impossible. The ques-

67

tion, therefore, is not one of intervention or nonintervention *per se* but of the ends and means of intervention."[16]

The absence of a clear understanding of the political purposes of foreign aid has generated a widespread feeling that our assistance to underdeveloped countries is an ill-conceived philanthropy that has nothing to do with the objectives of our foreign policy. As the Clay Committee expressed it, the American people are increasingly disposed to feel "that we are trying to do too much for too many too soon, that we are overextended in resources and under-compensated in results, and that no end of foreign aid is either in sight or in mind."[17]

We must make a major new effort, in close cooperation with our Atlantic allies, to define specific as well as general objectives in foreign aid, to distinguish clearly between what it can and cannot be expected to accomplish, and to reshape our aid programs accordingly. A new approach, it seems to me, must be in the direction of rigorous *selectivity* —selectivity as to whom we will help and how we will help them. We must evaluate such factors as the ability of a recipient to absorb capital, the presence or absence of trained personnel, the capacity for social reforms, and, above all, the potential contribution of the recipient to world peace and stability. In the words of the Clay Report: "Substantial tightening up and sharpened objectives in terms of our national interests are necessary, based on a realistic look at past experience, present needs, and future probabilities."[18] Or in Walter Lippmann's succinct phrase: "Let the bridges we have to build be fewer but let all of them cross the river."[19]

It is important that the West keep firm bearings on the over-all objective of its assistance to the poor countries of the world, which, as I have suggested, is to help create a world environment in which free societies can survive and flourish. It is equally important that we interpret this objective in terms of historical rather than immediate prospects. We have reason and the right to hope that our assistance will contribute to the spread of free institutions in the world, but this is a long-term prospect, which has little if any chance of fulfillment in the immediate future. "It is idle," writes Robert Heilbroner, "to pretend that the West can be an effective model for the immediate economic and political development of the backward world. What we must hope and work for is to make it a model for their long-term evolution."[20]

The rigors of economic development for backward countries are such that we must expect protracted periods of instability and, in some cases, of authoritarian government. Economic development is a profoundly revolutionary force, involving the overturn of vested interests and traditional ways of doing things and requiring great sacrifices in the present for the promise of greater rewards in the future. "There is no doubt," writes Eric Hoffer, "that individual freedom is an unequaled factor in the release of social energies. . . . But this source of energy can be tapped only under special conditions: a society must be strong enough to support, and affluent enough to afford, individual freedom. It would thus be wholly unreasonable to expect a backward country to modernize itself in a hurry in an atmosphere of freedom. Its poverty, lack of skill, and its need for fervor and unity militate against it."[21]

The West, with its radically different kind of experience, is only beginning to perceive that the ascent from poverty in Asia, Africa, and Latin America involves the revolutionary transformation of societies and that there is little possibility of achieving this transformation through the methods of Western political democracy. The basic requirement for economic growth is of course capital; and in desperately poor countries, except for limited assistance from outside, capital can only be formed by forced savings, that is, by holding down or further lowering levels of consumption that are barely above subsistence. The rigorous discipline and harsh controls that this involves have already led in some countries and is likely to lead in others to the displacement of parliamentary systems by authoritarian regimes.

It is an unanswered question whether the West, especially the United States, is prepared to assist and support for long periods regimes which do not pursue policies of democratic capitalism. My own view is that we must recognize the exigencies of development, however distasteful they may be, and lend our support to those governments which meet three main tests: first, that they have the will and capacity for economic growth; secondly, that they pursue policies which infringe on popular liberties only to the extent absolutely necessary for the country's development plans; and, thirdly, that they are committed to the establishment of democratic institutions at the earliest practicable time.

I believe such an approach to be consistent with our objective of shaping a concert of free nations. It requires us, in Robert Heilbroner's words, "to distinguish between mere oppression and oppressive but purposeful discipline, between static dictatorship and dictatorial development."[22] In short, we must take a calculated risk in supporting governments which, whatever their present character, seem likely in the long run to achieve both economic growth and political democracy and, in so doing, to contribute to our own long-term purposes.

Success in so difficult and delicate an enterprise is far more likely if the Western nations to the greatest possible extent remove their development efforts from domestic political arenas and channel them through international agencies. A unified Western effort in the field of foreign aid would serve the double purpose of creating new bonds between the Western nations themselves and of giving them a far more effective means of influencing the course of the underdeveloped world than they now have in their separate programs of aid. Indeed, if the Atlantic nations are prepared to accept the burden of generous, concerted, and long-term assistance to the more promising of the underdeveloped countries, then they can, I believe, make a powerful, and perhaps decisive, contribution to the creation of a peaceful and stable world environment.

The unification of Western aid programs will have meaning and effect only if every member of the Atlantic community accepts its fair share of the burden. Unfortunately only a very few of the prosperous countries of the free world have thus far accepted foreign aid responsibilities commensurate with their resources. I think it not improper to point out that although the United States is able and willing to bear its just share of the burden of aid to the poor nations and of the heavier burden of free world defense as well, it cannot carry indefinitely a disproportionate share when other nations, with equally much at stake, are reluctant to accept responsibilities commensurate with their strength.

As important as the amounts of Western development loans to the less-developed countries are the terms on which they are extended. If they are to serve their purpose of generating economic growth, these loans must be provided with long repayment periods and at substantially less than commercial rates of interest. In this respect as well as in the over-all scope of assistance, the United States has made a more significant effort than most other Western countries.

In the last decade the national income of the Atlantic countries has grown by at least 3 percent a year. It is their declared intention to add to it another $500 billion in the next decade. The poorer countries, by contrast, are barely managing to hold their own, and in some cases there have been sharp declines. Given this contrast, none of the prosperous Western nations can plead inability.

The political stakes of Atlantic aid to the poor nations are nothing less than whether the Atlantic world is to be an isolated bastion of freedom and prosperity or the vital core of a world-wide concert of free nations. If we are to achieve the latter, we must concert our policies as to the amounts and duration, the priorities and methods of our aid. This is likely to require something more than the coordination of separate national aid programs. Because bargaining between states often produces only a smallest common denominator of agreed action, it is possible that we shall eventually have to apply to our aid programs some such political procedures as those which have proven so effective in the European Economic Community. As Lord Franks has put it: "A new way has to be found: a new organization, institution or commission, which will have sufficient standing, independence and initiative to formulate common solutions and put them forward to the governments of the several nations of the group, so that they will have to face in argument not merely each other but also and at the same time the solution proposed for the partnership as a whole as best realizing its common good."[23]

My own belief is that the "new way" called for by Lord Franks can be developed through existing international machinery. One can envision the development of a unified multilateral aid program through either the International Development Association of the World Bank or the Development Assistance Committee of the OECD, or through the use of both of these agencies.

The International Development Association was brought into existence for the express purpose of serving as the principal international instrument for the provision of long-term development loans at low rates of interest. It has the advantages of highly competent administration and of objectivity on political matters that are extraneous to economic development. As Eugene Black has pointed out, the World Bank and the International Development Association are uniquely qualified to grant or deny loans on their merits. "Because they are known to have no ulterior motive," he has said, "they can exert more influence over the use of a loan than is possible for a bilateral lender: they can insist that the projects for which they lend are established on a sound basis, and—most important—they can make their lending conditional upon commensurate efforts being made by the recipient country itself."[24]

As presently constituted, the Development Assistance Committee of the OECD has neither the administrative competence nor the scope and experience of the International Development Association. It is, however, a primarily Atlantic body, with a consequent potentiality for advancing the community of the West as well as the development of the poor countries. Composed of nearly all of the free nations that are capable of significant foreign aid efforts, the OECD and its Development Assistance Committee provide an institutional framework for economic partnership among Europe, Japan, and North America.

In time the Western nations may find that their common interest in the development of the poor nations has created an appropriate "function" to be discharged by an Atlantic executive organ with limited but clearly specified powers. Such a departure would raise delicate questions of national sovereignty and is not likely to be feasible in the near future. For the present we can do no more than to make the best possible use of the Development Assistance Committee for the coordination of national efforts. But as new attitudes evolve—if they evolve—we might consider the elevation of the Committee from a policy coordinating to a policy *making* body. Conceivably, the Committee could be empowered to make its decisions under a system of "qualified majority" voting like that of the Common Market Council of Ministers. Under this system it might be authorized to determine amounts and conditions of aid to be extended by the group, and also to determine appropriate contributions by the Atlantic countries. The latter determinations, of course, could not be binding "assessments," for obvious constitutional reasons, certainly in the United States. But the amounts set by the Committee might be expected to impose a considerable *moral* obligation upon the participating nations.

Whatever the forms and the instrumentalities that the rich nations use in their efforts to help the poor nations, and whatever the disappointments and reverses that are suffered in the process, we must at all times keep sight of the high stakes involved, of the hopes and opportunities that depend upon our success. In unity and common purpose, we have it within our power to shape a concert of free nations and, building thereon, to lead the world toward a new era of hope and progress. "Our age will be well remembered," said Arnold Toynbee, "not for its horrifying crimes or its astonishing inventions but because it is the first generation since the dawn of history in which mankind dared to believe it practical to make the benefits of civilization available to the whole human race."

.    .    .

IN ALL the problems confronting the Atlantic world—defense and trade, political cooperation and foreign aid—one simple but compelling theme prevails: the unity or division of free peoples. Since the age of discovery when the Atlantic community was formed, its members have periodically fallen upon one another with the increasingly savage instruments of their advancing military technology. So long as the North Atlantic nations dominated the world and so long as their weapons were of limited destructive power, the "civil war" of the West was endurable, though self-defeating. That time is now past. The Atlantic nations no longer dominate the world, nor could they expect to survive as organized societies a nuclear conflict with those who threaten them. History and reason and common sense tell us that unity is the condition for preventing such a conflict, that in unity lies our best hope of preserving the civilization we have built and of fulfilling its considerable promise.

75

# 3 · THE AMERICAN AGENDA

"IT IS provided in the very essence of things," wrote Walt Whitman, "that from any fruition of success, no matter what, shall come forth something to make a greater struggle necessary." By all the standards of history that measure the success of nations, America is at the flood tide of growth and achievement. We have become pre-eminent in world power and responsibility; we have created a society in which poverty is a lingering vestige rather than the normal condition of man; we have developed stable political institutions which, with all their imperfections, have proven adaptable to change and at the same time capable of preserving liberty and law. The problems that confront us issue directly from these achievements. They are no less compelling, no less fraught with danger, for being problems of success.

They may indeed be more dangerous because success breeds satisfaction and satisfaction breeds complacency and arrogance. "I'll say this for adversity," said Elbert Hubbard, "people seem to be able to stand it and that's more than can be said for prosperity." To the extent that we are mesmerized with the general success of our society, we are blinded to its particular shortcomings and to the opportunities that wealth and power have brought us. World power and domestic abundance are the great achievements of America. They are also its greatest dangers because neither power nor wealth is itself the condition of the good life. They are rather the preconditions, the instruments which, if forged to worthy ends, can open vistas of human excellence and fulfillment.

For the past generation we have been preoccupied with power. Our major energies have been dedicated to an enormously costly but generally successful struggle against Communist imperialism. We have made great sacrifices to sustain the struggle because of our profound conviction that our form of society was immeasurably superior to Communist society in its capacity to create the conditions of a happy and rewarding life. I believe that this global effort has been altogether necessary and justified, but I also believe that we have become so preoccupied with the struggle itself that we have largely lost sight of the issue at stake, which is the character and quality of two competing kinds of society. In our zeal to defend the American way of life, we have lost interest in its sustenance and improvement, permitting our priorities to become so inverted that the deterioration of our free society is accepted as the price of its defense.

At the same time, we have fallen into a state of benign satisfaction with affluence at home. Prosperity appears to have benumbed the social conscience which brought us the benefits we now enjoy. In our absorption with the pleasures of shiny new cars, of a thousand gadgets of trivial utility, and of the inexhaustible inanities of television, we hardly notice that over four million Americans are unemployed, that our public schools are deteriorating tragically, that crime and blight and corruption continue to spread over our cities. Still less are we inclined to ask ourselves whether

77

conspicuous consumption is really all we want of life, whether we are using our wealth in a way that truly satisfies us, whether there is something else to be done, something that we are not now doing, to fulfill the promise of America.

These problems are the products of past success, but they are also, if left unsolved, the raw materials for future failure. Whether and how we solve them has everything to do with the quality of our society and everything to do with its defense, because, as Kenneth Thompson has written, "military power is like the fist whose force depends on the health and vitality of the body politic and the whole society."[1] The distinction between foreign and domestic policy has largely disappeared. The resolution of long-neglected problems at home has as much to do with one as with the other, and, because this is so, they warrant first priority on the American agenda.

Although the tasks to be performed are formidable, the assets which we bring to them are great. We have first of all the processes of the oldest going constitutional system in the world. It has serious defects of inflexibility under the conditions of the twentieth century, but in the past it has demonstrated a capacity for timely response to the needs of a dynamic society, having failed only once to cope with an overriding national issue. We have in addition the prodigious assets of the most productive economy and the most efficient technology that the world has ever known. We have, above all, the human resources of a dynamic and creative population—a population endowed, in Eric Hoffer's words, "with a superb dynamism, an unprecedented diffusion of skills, a genius for organization and teamwork, a flexibility which makes possible an easy adjustment to the

78

most drastic change, an ability to get things done with a minimum of tutelage and supervision, an unbounded capacity for fraternization."[2]

The question that remains is how we are to use these formidable assets, whether we are to squander them in the traditional struggle for wealth and power as ends in themselves or use them to create a golden age of American civilization. Other nations have had this choice, and their decisions are instructive. Periclean Athens achieved the highest civilization of the ancient world and then brought ruin on itself and its civilization in the pursuit of military glory and conquest. Modern Germany developed a capacity to make an enduring contribution to civilization but cast it away when she chose instead to demonstrate her greatness by military adventures which ended in her ruin. I do not think it probable that the American people will embark on such a course, but neither do I think they fully understand the lesson of ancient Greece and modern Germany: that history judges the greatness of nations not for their power and conquests but for their creativity and their lasting contributions to civilization. "The great crusades of history," writes August Heckscher, "have passed by all but the tiniest minority of men; the lives of the vast majority received as much of beauty as they held from the quality of their particular civilization."[3]

Men do not as a general practice question their lives and values when all is seemingly going well or face their problems before they are overwhelmed by them. "No one can have lived in the world," wrote Spinoza, "without observing that most people, when in prosperity, are so overbrimming with wisdom . . . that they take every offer of advice as a personal insult, whereas in adversity they know not where to turn, but beg and pray for counsel from every passer-by."[4] The question before the American people is whether, without awaiting adversity, they are prepared to examine the foundations of their power and prosperity, to question the priorities of public policy, and, in so doing, to determine whether the course which they are now following is in fact the one which is most likely to gain security from power and happiness from wealth.

．　　　．　　　．

OF ALL the national enterprises in which our country is currently engaged, none, apparently, has stirred the interest and imagination of the people more than the exploration of outer space. With little hesitation and debate we have committed ourselves to an enormously costly space program, including a $20 billion project for landing an American on the moon before 1970 and—what is more important—ahead of the Russians. Since the experts agree that the moon has no foreseeable value as a military base, we are doing this because we believe it essential to our prestige.

"Prestige," in Webster's definition, is the "power to command admiration." Among the questions which present themselves about the high priority which is attached to space exploration, the most obvious is whether "prestige"— the "power to command admiration"—is in fact pre-eminent among our national needs. Assuming that it is, are we quite certain that being "first in space" will insure our prestige or, obversely, if the Russians reach the moon ahead of us, that we will lose the admiration of the world and become "second-rate people" in the eyes of the world and in our own eyes as well? Are there not other factors involved in our prestige and self-esteem, such as our capacity to employ and educate, to house and transport our own people? If, at the end of this decade, the Russians should have reached the moon and we should not, but have instead succeeded in the renovation of our cities and of our transport, in the virtual elimination of slums and crime, in the creation of the best system of public education in the world, whose prestige would be higher, who more admired by the world? Is it not possible, if we were to do these things, that our prestige and influence would reach unprecedented heights in a world that is hungry for education, for a decent material life, and for human dignity?

The issue is one of priorities. The question is not whether space exploration is desirable in itself but whether it is a more important and pressing national need than other needs such as employment and education and urban renewal, which are given much lower priority by both the executive and legislative branches of the federal government.

The rebuttal that is offered to suggestions that education, welfare, and economic development should be given priority over space is a political one. It is contended that we did not spend enough money on these worthwhile purposes before we had a space program and that there is no assurance that we would increase our efforts in these areas if the space program were abandoned or reduced. This seems to me partly but not entirely accurate. The Congress has come close on several occasions to adopting a meaningful program of federal aid to education, and it is quite possible that the reduction of costs in other areas such as space would provide the necessary impetus for the enactment of an education bill. In any case, I find the negative argument that we would not in any case use funds that now go into space for other constructive purposes a singularly unconvincing reason for the expenditure of vast sums of public money. This argument itself, in my opinion, strengthens the case for greater efforts in education.

The manpower requirements for space research are enormous, and it is difficult to see how they can be met without drawing scientists and engineers away from other fields where there is already a shortage of trained personnel. Indeed, far from drawing manpower from among the four million unemployed, space research requires the scientific and engineering talent which is most urgently needed in fields of civilian technology. In addition, it is quite possible that the program of graduate fellowships through which the National Aeronautics and Space Administration hopes to help meet its manpower needs will draw an excessive number of students from the humanities into science and from basic scientific research into space technology.

The mind does not readily grasp the significance of a sum of 20 billion dollars, the projected cost of landing an American on the moon. Its meaning, I think, can be shown through some simple statistics. Twenty billion dollars over a ten-year period is $5\frac{1}{2}$ million dollars a day. According to official calculations of the costs of school construction, a single day's costs for the moon program, that is, $5\frac{1}{2}$ million dollars, could be used to build five schools for 1,000 students each, 25 schools for 200 students each, or 50 schools for 100 students each. The amount expended in one month on the moon program would pay for 375 schools with 400 students each, or 750 schools with 200 students each.

I am puzzled by other aspects of space exploration. It is apparent that military communications satellites are making an important contribution to our national security, but I, for one, am unable to understand the urgency of our need for a civilian communications satellite system. This, however, was the subject of an acrimonious debate in the United States Senate in the summer of 1962, a debate which occupied an inordinate amount of the Senate's time and energy, certainly a great deal more than such matters as education and slum clearance. The Telstar communications satellite is of course a splendid scientific achievement and it will undoubtedly be a fine thing when television broadcasts can be viewed simultaneously in London, Paris, and New York. But is this really a matter of urgency? Is it such an intolerable hardship for Europeans to have to wait twenty-four hours while video tapes of American quiz shows and horse operas are flown across the Atlantic in jet planes?

The question is not, as I have said, whether we should or should not have a space program but what priority it should have in relation to pressing and long-neglected national needs. The problem was very adequately expressed by Dr. James R. Killian, Jr., Chairman of the Corporation of M.I.T. and former science adviser to the President, in a speech he made as long ago as December 13, 1960. He said he was not opposed to sending men into space but the American people must face the question of whether the rate at which the program was then proceeding would weaken other national programs, including defense. He said, "They must face up to the tough decision as to whether we can justify billions of dollars for man in space when our educational system is so inadequately supported," and he asked,

"Will several billion dollars a year additional for enhancing the quality of education not do more for the future of the United States and its position in the world than several billion dollars a year additional for man in space?"

Without doubt the winner in the race to the moon will have great prestige for a time and will be widely regarded as the nation which rides the wave of the future. But when the second and third men follow the first man on the moon, the glory will fade and the race may seem far less significant than it did before. In any case, the race to the moon, whatever its outcome, will not decide the course of history. Its true meaning, I think, is expressed in a story that is told of a Russian pupil in a physics class, who, when told of the plans to land a Russian on the moon, agreed that this was a fine thing and asked: "But when may we go to Vienna?"

.    .    .

MORE LIKELY to have a lasting effect on history will be the success or failure of the United States in solving the problem of full employment in an expanding economy.

". . . the United States," wrote William Graham Sumner in the 1880's, "is the great country for the unskilled laborer. The economic conditions all favor that class. There is a great continent to be subdued and there is a fertile soil available to labor, with scarcely any need of capital. Hence the people who have strong arms have what is most needed."[5]

Even when Sumner wrote these words the process of rapid industrialization was underway which was to create the diametrically opposite situation of our own time. The American economy of the 1960's is fueled by capital and technology, and by scientists and technicians and highly skilled workers. Unskilled labor is rapidly becoming super-fluous as a factor of production, and the untrained and uneducated worker, of whom there are still some millions in the United States, finds himself increasingly relegated to a life of unemployment and underemployment, a life of diminishing rewards, diminishing hopes, and growing dis-illusion with our society.

While we continue to neglect public education, the correlation between unemployment and lack of education continues to mount. Of the 4.1 million Americans who were unemployed in March 1959, one million, or about one fourth of the total, had less than an elementary school education; and 2.8 million, or more than two thirds, had less than a high school education. In March 1961 the unemployment rate among professional and technical workers was 1.6 percent; among clerical workers, 4.9 per-cent; skilled workers, 9.1 percent; semi-skilled workers, 12.1 percent; and unskilled workers, 19.1 percent.

Under these conditions, the prospects are bleak indeed for the 42 percent of all American teen-agers who fail to complete high school. There is no longer a western frontier to which they can migrate. There is no need for more farmers, and even if there were, the drop-outs from school could not qualify because modern American farming re-quires highly developed skills. Nor are very many of the drop-outs likely to be absorbed by industrial expansion, even rapid expansion if it should occur, because industrial productivity expands primarily by the use of automated machines which reduce the need for unskilled labor. Be-tween 1956 and 1961, for example, the productive capacity of the steel industry increased by 20 percent, but the number of workers required to operate the industry's plants at full capacity dropped by 17,000. In the same period the increasingly automated chemical industry expanded by 27 percent while the number of production jobs fell by 3 percent.

Inadequate education represents a reckless squandering of the nation's human resources. Studies of high school drop-outs show that 70 percent of these young people have at least average intelligence and could complete high school and that 6 to 13 percent are of superior intelligence and fully capable of doing college work. Were these young people educated to their fullest capacity, they would have every chance of becoming responsible and productive citizens. The failure to educate them causes a major loss of economic productivity and incalculable personal and social problems—and therefore a heavy drain on the over-all strength of the nation.

Whatever the prospects for economic expansion and the reduction of unemployment by tax reduction and fiscal policy, the future holds little hope for those with only their muscle power to sell. Unemployment is a challenge not just to economic and fiscal policy, which can go far toward alleviating it. To at least as great a degree, it is a challenge to our educational system—a challenge that is not now being met. Through such legislation as the National Defense Education Act of 1958, Congress has provided a measure of support for higher education in such fields as science, engineering, and languages. But for the 80 percent of American youth who do not go to college, Congress has repeatedly failed to take meaningful action. Throughout the country, but especially in the relatively poor states such as my own, millions of young people are consigned to suffer the consequences of inadequate general education and grossly inadequate vocational training.

"The biggest failure of American education," writes Edward T. Chase, a student of the social and political effects of automation, "is not its inability to produce more scientists than Russia. It is the way in which it is turning millions of young people into unemployables."[6] A scant $7 million a year is provided for federal support of vocational education under the Smith-Hughes Act of 1917, and this goes primarily for training in agriculture and home economics. In a national economy in which farm employment continues to decline, in which no more than one applicant in ten can hope to find employment on a farm when he leaves school, this is indeed training for unemployment.

Constructive but limited measures to support vocational education have been taken through the adoption of the Area Redevelopment Act of 1961 and the Manpower Development and Training Act of 1962. These programs are valuable as far as they go, but that is not very far. Involving pitifully small numbers of young people, they scarcely begin to cope with the problem of training our youth for employment.

General unemployment rises slowly over long periods, but the number of young people out of work is mounting rapidly. This is largely the result of the gross imbalance of an educational system which neglects the vast majority of its youth who do not go to college. Such inadequate vocational education as exists is low in quality and grossly

87

imbalanced in its focus, producing unneeded farmers and neglecting such fields as auto mechanics and electrical service where demand is rising and skills are in short supply.

"Today," writes Edward T. Chase, "rational education must include training for the 80 percent of all young Americans who enter the labor market without college degrees. To ignore their vocational training is a reverse twist on the Eskimos' fabled custom of pushing their unproductive senior citizens onto the ice pack. That practice at least has a certain economic logic. Our system is managing to be at once inhumane and economically suicidal."[7]

The *Manpower Report of the President,* transmitted to the Congress in March 1963, makes it clear beyond doubt that we are failing to cope with the problem of unemployment, that indeed the situation is slowly deteriorating. In each of the recovery periods following the four postwar recessions unemployment has stuck at a higher level than before. From a postwar low of 2.6 percent of the labor force in the wake of the recession of 1948–49, unemployment fell only to 3.9 percent after the 1953–54 downturn, to 5 percent after the 1957–58 recession, and to 5.3 percent after the recession of 1960–61. The long-term trend is thus toward ever-increasing unemployment. This prodigal waste of human resources is costing us enormous sums in loss of productivity each year, to say nothing of its costs in human suffering, in blight and crime and juvenile delinquency.

The reversal of this trend depends in part on economic expansion, but primarily on education. Even with over 4 million Americans unemployed, there are shortages of qualified workers in science, engineering, teaching, health,

88

and other professional fields. These are fields which are permanently closed to the unskilled and the undereducated.

The present problem is the result of past successes. It is a cruel paradox that high unemployment is a price which Americans are paying for their own efficiency and productivity. The "economic miracle" of Europe and Japan, where there is little or no unemployment, has obscured the fact that an American factory worker produces three times as much as a European, seven times as much as a Japanese. Unemployment, though largely a result of our great advances in productivity and automation, is nonetheless a problem which, if left unsolved, will turn strength into weakness, success into failure. It has everything to do with our prosperity at home and with the success of our policies abroad and, far more than the moon and outer space, it has implications for the course of history.

.        .        .

"THE ESTABLISHMENT of republican government," wrote Horace Mann, "without well-appointed and efficient means for the universal education of the people, is the most rash and foolhardy experiment ever tried by man . . . It may be an easy thing to make a republic, but it is a very laborious thing to make republicans; and woe to the republic that rests upon no better foundations than ignorance, selfishness and passion! Such a republic may grow in numbers and in wealth . . . Its armies may be invincible, and its fleets may strike terror into nations on the opposite side of the globe at the same hour. Vast in its extent and enriched with all the prodigality of Nature it may possess every capacity and opportunity of being great and of doing good. But, if such a republic be devoid of intelligence, it will only the more closely resemble an obscene giant who has waxed strong in his youth and grown wanton in his strength; whose brain has been developed only in the region of the appetites and passions . . . Such a republic, with all its noble capacities for beneficence, will rush with the speed of a whirlwind to an ignominious end . . ."[8]

Beyond the vocational and professional responsibilities of public education lies its broad responsibility for shaping the character of a free people, for training the citizens of a free society to meet the heavy responsibilities of a democracy, to develop it into an instrument of progress and civilization rather than the "obscene giant" described by Horace Mann. In this respect as in the case of vocational instruction, I do not believe that the American educational system is meeting its responsibilities. The problem, I believe, is the foremost of our national life, one which is now ranked low but warrants pre-eminence on the American agenda.

The challenge to our education is both quantitative and qualitative. The quantitative problem is essentially one of providing adequate funds for improving the physical plants of our schools and for providing adequate training and salaries for teachers. Because of the tremendous differences among the states in income, wealth, and taxpaying ability, there can be no satisfactory solution to this problem except through a program of federal aid to education, without federal controls. Even with confiscatory tax rates, the poorest states and the poorest districts would be unable to finance public school systems of the quality that our young people deserve and the national welfare requires.

Education is a national problem which requires national solutions. Because of the mobility of our people and the interdependence of every element of our national economy, an inadequate school system in any one state adversely affects the entire nation. The federal government is uniquely qualified to raise the money needed to finance improvements in local school systems, and its obligation to do so derives from the fact that the entire nation suffers when any of our citizens are denied the best possible education.

A program of federal aid to education can and should be governed by strict safeguards against federal control. I appreciate the fears of those who believe that federal aid inevitably will lead to control, but I think that past experience has proven these fears to be unfounded. We have in fact had federal aid—without controls—since the earliest days of the Republic, starting with the Land Ordinances of 1785 and 1787, which gave millions of acres of land to the states for education. The Morrill Act of 1862 helped establish land grant colleges such as the University of Arkansas. The GI bills of World War II and the Korean War helped millions of veterans to obtain education and, most recently, the National Defense Education Act of 1958 has provided many forms of aid to schools and to individual students. The experience of these and other programs offers convincing evidence that federal aid to education is necessary as well as beneficial and that it is compatible with the retention of full direction and control by local communities.

Although our expenditures on public education have risen rapidly in the last decade, they have not nearly kept pace with the increase in our school-age population, which since 1950 has grown twice as fast as the total population. We have in effect "economized" on education and for this false economy the nation is paying an appalling price, a price that permeates every area of our national life, both at home and abroad.

Quite as important as the problem of adequate support for education, and even more difficult to solve, is the problem of quality and content.

"Governments reflect human nature," said Plato. "States are not made out of stone or wood, but of the character of their citizens: these turn the scale and draw everything after them."[9] Those words, I think, define the challenge to education in our free society—the development of character in the individual, which in turn determines our national character, and, therefore, our national destiny.

"If a nation expects to be ignorant and free in a state of civilization," said Jefferson, "it expects what never was and never will be."[10] The preservation of our free society in the years and decades to come will depend ultimately on whether we succeed or fail in directing the enormous power of human knowledge to the enrichment of our own lives and to the shaping of a rational and civilized world order. In the twentieth century the world has become united in the purely physical sense of economic and technological interdependence, while in psychological and spiritual terms it remains divided into suspicious and hostile national communities. It is the task of education, more than of any other instrument of public policy, to help close the dangerous gap between the economic and technological interdependence of the peoples of the world and their psychological, political, and spiritual alienation.

What kind of education can be expected to meet so formidable a challenge? I do not presume to know the answer to this question, but in general it seems to me that an adequate system of education for our time is one which concentrates above all on the cultivation of the free spirit and the free mind, one which aims to teach men not *what* to think but *how* to think. As Admiral H. G. Rickover has put it: "Among the valuable fruits of a good *liberal* education is capacity to gauge the long range consequences of one's personal acts, a sense of responsibility to the larger community for these acts, a concern for the future and the fate of one's descendants."[11]

American education is not at present realizing these objectives. I do not suggest that our system of education is a failure but that, despite its impressive achievements on every level, it is falling short both of its own promise and of our national needs. The crisis in our education is not a matter of catching up with or outstripping the Russians in the number of engineers or scientists that we turn out each year. Indeed Soviet education, according to available evidence, is far inferior to ours except in certain fields of science and engineering.[12] The crisis is one which would confront us even if Communism and the Soviet Union did not exist. It is a crisis of our own character as a free society and the ability of a free society to bring meaning and fulfillment to the lives of its citizens.

Our constant objective in education must be the cultivation of the free mind—the mind which is free of dogma, cant, and superstition, free to fulfill the highest measure of its capacity, free to explore the limitless realm of ideas and values. Such an education must be pre-eminently con-

93

cerned with standards of excellence. In the words of Ralph Barton Perry: "As the debasing of standards to the level of the mass is the besetting weakness of democracy, so a clear and uncompromising definition of standards is its first educational duty. Democratic education should be an education *up* and not an education *down*—in all its stages. It will always ask more than it gets and develop capacity by straining it. It will encourage rather than congratulate."[13]

Throughout our history we have had both an intense belief in education and, along with it, a paradoxical strand of anti-intellectualism. Samuel Butler took note of the same tendency with regard to religion when he wrote: "People in general are equally horrified at hearing the Christian religion doubted, and at seeing it practiced."[14] In fact, the anti-intellectual strain is inherent in the *kind* of faith we put in education. We have placed too little emphasis on the training of the intellect and too much on such marginal values as being an "interesting" or "well-adjusted" or "well-rounded" person—or almost anything except creativeness. We have viewed higher education too little as the means of elevating the mind and spirit and too much as the road to "know-how" and "success" through the mastery of technical and practical fields of knowledge. In so doing, we have neglected the kind of education that develops the capacity to handle general ideas and to sift the irrational from the rational.

There have been two ideals in American educational thought, the "Jeffersonian" concept of maintaining exacting standards and the "Jacksonian" concept of universality. I do not see why we cannot realize both of these ideals, making it possible for every American to be educated to the fullest measure of his capacity.

94

The overemphasis on the technical and practical does not mean that we should revert to a one-sided curriculum of classical and theoretical studies. Our education must challenge the capacities of all our citizens, honoring both scholarship and artisanship, both theory and technique. The objective must be the pursuit of excellence and pride of achievement in all socially useful fields. Every citizen of a democracy should be encouraged to take pride in educational achievement, regardless of whether his capacity enables him to be a nuclear physicist or an automobile mechanic, a classical scholar or a skilled laborer.

The unfulfilled task of American education is to train the free individual to realize the worthiest possibilities of his freedom and, in so doing, to bring to bear the full weight of knowledge and wisdom on the solution of our national problems. "What belongs in education," writes Robert Hutchins, "is what helps the student to learn to think for himself, to form an independent judgment, and to take his part as a responsible citizen."[15] This includes, among other things, the development of the critical faculties. It would be quite as consistent with the American value system to offer prizes for the most penetrating criticisms of our country as for the most perceptive expressions of patriotism. The core of democracy is freedom of thought and expression, of which independent criticism is the indispensable element.

The object of liberal education is wisdom. The core of its curriculum, accordingly, should be composed of the classical disciplines that contribute to the rigorous training of the mind—the physical sciences and mathematics; languages and the arts; history, economics, and the theory and practice of government.

A society can be no better than the individuals who compose it and education is the crucible for the improvement of the individual. As George Washington wrote: "Knowledge is in every country the surest basis of public happiness. In one in which the measures of government receive their impressions so immediately from the sense of the community as in ours, it is proportionately essential."[16]

It is the responsibility of education to equip the American people for valid perceptions of the real world of the twentieth century, to liberate them from the peculiar limitations of the American perspective. "Changes in national thought," said a distinguished historian, "occur not by mutation but by evolution. Old ideas do not suddenly become obsolete; rather they gradually become irrelevant. And in all societies people are slow to discover the irrelevance of their traditional vocabulary."[17]

If we are to meet the dangers and to realize the opportunities of a continually changing world, it is essential that we discard those elements of our "traditional vocabulary" which have become irrelevant, that we develop a greater capacity than we now have to accept change and to cope with its consequences.

We must learn to understand the revolutionary upheavals of the twentieth century not in terms of illusory and egocentric analogies to our own experience but rather as the products of social forces quite new in the world, social forces that have no parallel in American experience. We are, as Louis Hartz has pointed out, an unrevolutionary society in a revolutionary world, a nation which was "born free" and which, except for a tragic Civil War, grew to maturity under circumstances of comfort, satisfaction, and continuous success.[18] We have known little indeed, compared to other peoples, of the anguish and oppression which unleashed the revolutionary forces of the twentieth century. Nevertheless, we have not yet acknowledged the limitations of our perspective or accepted the proposition that our proper task is not to try to reshape the world in the American image but to lend such support as we can, moral and material, to peoples who face overwhelming problems of a character and intensity that we have never known.

The uniqueness of American experience and our pride in unexampled achievements has contributed to a strand of American thought and character which fosters the periodic rise of movements based on intolerance. That strand of thought lies deep in our past. It underlay the "alien and sedition" laws of the 1790's, the "know-nothing" movement of the 1850's, the McCarthyism of the 1950's, and the radical right-wing organizations of the last few years. The genesis of the radical right movement of our own time, like that of its predecessors, is the psychic heritage of a nation which was "born free," a nation which, having experienced virtual unanimity as to basic forms and values, is inclined at times to regard unfamiliar opinions with intolerance and revulsion, confusing dissent with disloyalty. This frame of mind hampers creative action abroad by identifying the alien with the unintelligible and it inspires hysteria at home by generating the anxiety which unintelligible things produce.

I for one do not believe that the "American Proposition" has validity for the entire world, though it is eminently valid for America. Its limitations are defined by the uniqueness of our political heritage and by the limitations of our material resources. We must learn that the methods and approaches that have worked so well for us will not necessarily work for peoples with radically different heritages and resources, who perforce must forge their own political institutions—institutions which we hope will be dedicated to freedom and democracy, but which must be rooted in the special characters and heritages of the peoples whom they serve.

The problem was stated admirably by Mark Twain in his essay, "To the Person Sitting in Darkness," in which he asked: ". . . shall we go on conferring our Civilization upon the peoples that sit in darkness, or shall we give those poor things a rest? Shall we bang right ahead in our old-time, loud, pious way, and commit the new century to the game; or shall we sober up and sit down and think it over first?"

We Americans will have learned the fundamental lessons of liberal education when we fully grasp that it is not possible to reshape the world in the American image. The modern West of which we are the leader represents one, but not the only, valid form of human civilization. There is no validity to the ancient Hebraic idea of a "chosen people" or to the Hegelian concept that in every era one leading nation represents the spirit of the age. History is too complex to be explained by such simple doctrines. The world revolution of our time for the most part involves peoples who do not wish—or whose history and traditions do not incline them—to accept the "American way of life." There is no reason for despair over this fact, for the world is enriched by intellectual and cultural diversity.

The task of broadening the perspective of American

thought is the unfulfilled task of education. If our schools and universities are to meet this challenge, they must above all remain true to themselves. The university professor must bring to his profession an unwavering consciousness of his responsibility to his students, an active awareness that every lecture, every book and article is helping to shape the mind of America. The university professor who comes to government should come as a professor, with pride in his profession and with a clear understanding of his role as one who brings ideas and ideals and a broad perspective to an arena in which they are often lacking. He is needed in government as a thinker and not as a political practitioner; he is needed to do the serious reflection about long-range problems which we professional politicians so often fail to do. He is *not* needed as an extra participant in the bargaining and manipulating processes of politics. These are the functions of professional politicians, of whom there is no shortage in Washington.

In an age of world-wide upheaval and nuclear weapons we must learn to conduct our affairs, foreign and domestic, with patience and tolerance, with breadth of view and a sense of history. These are qualities of educated men. Their cultivation is the ultimate challenge to education.

· · ·

EACH of the major issues of American life is by itself enormously complex and difficult to resolve. When one issue, such as education, is complicated by the introduction of other issues, such as race or religion, the resulting complexities and controversies are likely to lead to general paralysis and failure.

99

I do not suggest that education and race relations are unrelated to each other; on the contrary, they are profoundly related. Unfortunately, however, they are being linked with each other in a negative and destructive way, in a way which prevents progress in one unless there is simultaneous and equivalent progress in the other. By making our public schools the arena for the highly emotional issue of race, we have generated unnecessary passions and animosities which aggravate race relations and at the same time add an enormous obstacle to our efforts to improve public education. The tragedy of this situation is that the merger of issues has self-defeating results. Instead of generating progress in race relations through progress in education we have inserted the passions of race into an inadequate system of education and thereby foreclosed, or at least reduced, progress in both.

The irony is that if education and race relations were linked together in a constructive and positive relationship the result could be substantial advances in both. Education, I believe, is the *precondition,* the indispensable precondition, for the resolution of problems of race. It is axiomatic that prejudices and injustices relating to race are the product of ignorance. Only through the processes of education can men of different races learn to live together in harmony and in full respect for each other's rights.

The people of the South, including my own state of Arkansas, are burdened with an historical legacy that the rest of the nation does not share. They are marked in some ways by a strange disproportion inherited from the age of Negro slavery. The white person and the Negro of Arkansas and the South are equally prisoners of their environment and no one knows what either of them might have been in a different environment or under other circumstances. Certainly, neither of them has ever been free with respect to racial relationship to the degree that the New Englander has been free. The society of each is conditioned by the presence of the other. In the South one finds a relationship among men without counterpart on this continent. All this is the legacy of an ancient and melancholy history.

The issue of race relations in the South is part of the broader question of the relationship of the South to the nation as a whole. The legacy of Reconstruction, of political vindictiveness and the economic exploitation of the agricultural South by the industrial North, has only begun to fade in recent decades. Only since the 1930's has the South begun to share in the prosperity and affluence of America. Only since that time have we begun to be drawn—have we been allowed to be drawn—into the political, economic, and cultural life of the nation as a whole.

When, as occurred in April 1963, the United States Civil Rights Commission recommends the punitive withholding of federal funds from a Southern state, it calls forth the most bitter of the memories of the South, treating the South as an alien land rather than trying to draw it closer into the life of the nation as a whole. By aggravating poverty and inadequate education and economic opportunity, such a measure as the withholding of funds would contribute to the very conditions which generate racial tensions. The results of such an approach, an approach based on vindictiveness rather than reason, can only be inimical to the goals which it purports to advance.

If the problem of race relations is ever to be resolved in America—and I believe it will—its resolution will come about by the slow conversion of the human heart through the healing processes of education and not by remedies of a more urgent nature.

.    .    .

AMONG the problems which warrant high priority on the national agenda is the condition of our cities and the character and quality of urban life in America.

The great cities of America are beset with mounting problems of blight and crime, of inadequate financial resources, of traffic congestion and mass transport, of inadequate areas of open space and recreation, and even of a lack of pure air to breathe.

It has been suggested that the pressures of urban living will lead to a daily life divided into four distinct six-hour periods. Six hours a day will be spent in our automobiles—three in the morning going to work and three in the evening going home. Another six hours will be spent on the job, watching automated machines do the work, and perhaps the thinking, that formerly was done by men. The third six-hour period will be spent watching television, leaving us six hours for the rest of life, including sleep. The daytime schedule will of course require an adequate supply of tranquilizers, and sleeping pills will be required at night.

It need not come to this. There are many things that can be done, some of which are already being done—although on an inadequate scale—to bring order and serenity and beauty into an urban civilization.

One problem that can and should be solved within the

near future is that of mass transport. At present, traffic congestion in our cities is costing the nation some billions of dollars a year in losses of time, wages, and business, and in traffic accidents. In addition, congestion discourages private investment in the revitalization of cities and exacts a heavy price in the exhaustion of physical and emotional energies. The enactment by Congress of legislation to assist the financing of mass urban transport can relieve much of the congestion of the cities by helping to provide clean, rapid, and efficient mass transportation that will induce people to leave their automobiles at home. The result could be to make city streets safer and cleaner and to make it possible to preserve parks and such open areas as remain.

The multiplication of automobiles and trucks in cities has resulted in the retardation of transportation as well as in mounting costs. According to a traffic study made in 1907, horsedrawn vehicles in New York moved at an average speed of 11.5 miles an hour. Today automobiles crawl along the streets of New York at an average daytime speed of 6 miles an hour.[19]

Beyond this, congestion has deprived our cities of beauty and charm and style. "Such form as the metropolis achieves," writes Lewis Mumford, "is crowd form: the swarming bathing beach by the sea or the body of spectators in the boxing arena or the football stadium. With the increase of private motor cars, the streets and avenues become parking lots, and to move traffic at all, vast expressways gouge through the city and increase the demand for further parking lots and garages. In the act of making the core of the metropolis accessible, the planners of congestion have already almost made it uninhabitable."[20]

The United States has become a predominantly urban society. Over 70 percent of our people now live in cities. Some 95 percent of our recent population growth has occurred in metropolitan urban areas; it is estimated that in the next twenty years our urban areas will gain another 100 million people.

We shall need greatly improved mass transportation between as well as within cities, especially within the great east coast urban belt between Boston and Washington, D. C. At present a train trip between many American cities means an uncomfortable ride in a depressing coach and the near certainty of a tardy arrival. The litter and decay of the once beautiful Union Station in Washington could only have been achieved, in the judgment of the *Washington Post,* by a "full-time Department of Neglect."[21] I think there is great merit in a proposal made by Senator Pell of Rhode Island for the creation of a multi-state public authority which would be authorized to issue tax-exempt bonds to finance the modernization of railroads and the installation of rapid and efficient service along the east coast urban belt.

The prospective rate of growth of metropolitan urban areas in the United States—50 million people per decade —means that we must add to our cities during the next ten years as much in housing, factories, transport, schools, hospitals, and everything else that goes into the making of a city, as this country developed between 1700 and 1900. Even more important, the growth of urban areas means mounting problems of decay and slums, crime and delinquency—problems that will demand enormous efforts in urban renewal and social services, in employment and, most of all, in education.

While great new dwelling areas have grown up on the fringes, the centers of many of our great cities have been falling into decay. Buildings fall into disuse and sources of tax money dry up, while slums spread over formerly good residential areas and civic responsibility gives way to social disorganization. The reversal of this baleful tendency will require large sums of money, large-scale and creative efforts in urban planning and architecture and in social work and education, and perhaps radical changes in existing patterns of local government so as to bring sprawling metropolitan areas into unified and rational political units. "We need a new image of order," writes Lewis Mumford, "which shall include the organic and personal, and eventually embrace all the offices and functions of man. Only if we can project that image shall we be able to find a new form for the city."[22]

If America is to turn its great wealth into human satisfactions and the enrichment of our civilization, one of our foremost tasks must be the rebuilding of our cities and the life of our cities. Instead of the functional but spiritually arid towers of steel and glass that now rise in the core of the cities, we need edifices that bring style and variety, charm and character and joy into urban life. Instead of the bleak vistas of gaudy signs and drive-ins that now disfigure the fringe areas of the great cities, we need parks and open spaces for healthful recreation and spiritual renewal. ". . . significant improvements," writes Mumford, "will come only through applying art and thought to the city's central concerns, with a fresh dedication to the cosmic and ecological processes that enfold all being. We must restore to the city the maternal, life-nurturing functions, the autonomous activities, the symbiotic associations that have long been neglected or suppressed. For the city should be an organ of love; and the best economy of cities is the care and culture of men."[23]

.      .      .

THE FINAL item which I would insert high on the American agenda is the need for re-evaluation of the traditional relationships between citizen and government in a changing America and a changing world.

One of the cherished beliefs of the American past was the assumption that no problem of government was beyond the competence and understanding of the average citizen. In the eighteenth and nineteenth centuries this theory of government by amateurs was tenable enough. It was tenable because military technology was relatively simple, because the role of the government in the economic order was small, because we stood far from the centers of stress and conflict in the world and our foreign relations were intermittent and uncomplicated.

This traditional relationship between the people and their government has been shattered in the twentieth century by the impact of powerful new forces. Perhaps the foremost of these is the pace of change itself. It took man 500,000 years to arrive at the agricultural revolution, when he began to plant and cultivate crops; another 25,000 years to achieve the industrial revolution; then only 200 years to reach the atomic age; and only another 15 years to come into the space age. As the pace of scientific and technological change accelerates, the human mind is caught in a widening gap between its perceptions and the realities of its environment. Most of our political problems now have to do with scientific and technological matters of great complexity, and we have become dependent on experts and specialists for the resolution of our most compelling national problems.

A second major factor in the unhinging of traditional relationships between people and government is the fact that we now live at the very center of the stresses and conflicts of world politics. Our foreign relations have become enormously dangerous and complicated, and we are preeminent in both power and responsibility in the world. Our foreign relations and our domestic life have become profoundly involved with each other, and much of the traditional distinction between the two has ceased to have meaning.

These considerations, combined with the more traditional problems inherent in a democratic system, compel us to examine closely and critically many of the traditional patterns of American government, and particularly the relationship between the people and their government in the shaping of foreign policy.

"Foreign politics," wrote Alexis de Tocqueville, "demand scarcely any of those qualities which a democracy possesses; and they require, on the contrary, the perfect use of almost all those faculties in which it is deficient . . . a democracy is unable to regulate the details of an important undertaking, to persevere in a design, and to work out its execution in the presence of serious obstacles. It cannot combine its measures with secrecy, and it will not await their consequences with patience. These are qualities which more especially belong to an individual, or to an aristocracy."[24]

The problem of a democratic foreign policy is one aspect of the more fundamental question of man's capacity for self-government. Classical democratic thought is rooted in the assumption of human goodness and reason as the foundation of government by the people. The history of the last century and a half has not borne this assumption out. Again and again, free societies, including our own, have acted foolishly or disastrously as a result of their own shortsightedness and irrationality. Our own experience, culminating in the two world wars of the twentieth century and the constant danger of a third conflict that would destroy our civilization, has gravely undermined—if it has not totally destroyed—the high democratic optimism of the eighteenth century. "The play is still on," writes Carl Becker, "and we are still betting on freedom of the mind, but the outcome seems now somewhat more dubious than it did in Jefferson's time, because a century and a half of experience makes it clear that men do not in fact always use their freedom of speech and of the press in quite the rational and disinterested way they are supposed to."[25]

The conflicts and upheavals of the twentieth century have thrown the democracies on the defensive throughout the world and generated powerful strains within the free Western societies themselves. There has developed what Walter Lippmann calls "a functional derangement of the relationship between the mass of the people and the government." "The people," he writes, "have acquired power which they are incapable of exercising, and the governments they elect have lost powers which they must recover if they are to govern." The impact of mass opinion on vital issues of war and peace, in Lippmann's analysis, is to impose a "massive negative" at critical junctures when new courses of policy are needed. He contends that public opinion, lagging disastrously behind the movement of events, forced a vindictive peace in 1919, then refused to act against a resurgent Germany in the interwar years, and finally was aroused to paroxysms of hatred and unattainable hopes in a Second World War that need never have occurred. The impact of public opinion, says Lippmann, has been nothing less than a "compulsion to make mistakes."[26]

For a politician who serves at the pleasure of his constituency, the course of prudence is to adhere to prevailing views. To be prematurely right is to court what, to the politician at least, is a premature retirement. We come at last to the ironic inversion of the classical democratic faith in the will of the people: public opinion fails to hold the politician to the course of wisdom and responsibility; and not only that, but to take the right course requires a singular act of courage on the part of the politician. A few might share the Wilsonian view that "There is nothing more honorable than to be driven from power because one was right." Far more prevalent is the outlook of Lloyd George, who on more than one occasion quite candidly rejected proposals whose merits he conceded on the grounds that he did not wish to be "crucified" at home.[27] In the Lloyd George view, which is a prototype (and not without some merit in my opinion), there is little glory and still less constructive purpose in being defeated for failing to do the impossible.

The problem before us is to find a more realistic balance between the people and their government so as to reconcile the requirements of an effective foreign policy with the preservation of democratic liberties. At present, I believe, we depend too heavily in our policy processes on the transitory preferences of public opinion. In so doing, we greatly underestimate the difficulty of the task of shaping policy. We fail to recognize as Professor Gabriel Almond has put it, that "foreign policy is a tapestry of infinite complexity, and even the experts can only hope to achieve familiarity with a part of its intricate designs."[28]

A distinction must be made between means and ends. The average citizen is no more qualified for the detailed administration of government than the average politician is qualified to practice medicine or to split an atom. But in the choice of basic goals, the fundamental moral judgments that shape the life of a society, the judgment of trained elites is no more valid than the judgment of an educated people. The knowledge of the navigator is essential to the conduct of a voyage, but his special skills have no relevance to the choice of whether to take the voyage and where we wish to go. The experience of modern times shows us that when the passengers take over the navigation of the ship, it is likely to go on the rocks. This does not mean that their chosen destination is the wrong one or that an expert would have made a better choice, but only that they are unlikely to get there without the navigator's guidance.

The need, in short, is for democracy in the shaping of basic foreign policy decisions and professionalism in their implementation. It is the proper function of the electorate as a whole to determine the outer limits of permissible government action, to determine the general direction in which foreign policy should move, and to render judgment on crucial decisions and major departures from traditional policy. Within these broad confines, it seems to me, the formulation and implementation of specific policies are a task for trained professionals. I am well aware that the principle of professionalism in the conduct of foreign policy runs counter to the strong feelings of many Americans. The alternative, however, as George Kennan has pointed out, is "diplomacy by dilettantism."

To return to my metaphor, we must guard against allowing the navigator to determine our destination, but we must allow him to steer the ship without amateur supervision of every turn of the wheel. A political leader is chosen because of his supposed qualifications for his job. If he is qualified, he should be allowed to carry it out according to his own best judgment. If his judgment is found defective by his electors, he can and should be removed. His constituents, however, must recognize that he has a duty to his office as well as to them and that their duty in turn is to fill the office but not to run it. We must distinguish between the functions of *representation* and *government,* requiring our elected leaders to represent us while allowing them to govern.

In a time of continuing international crisis with the danger of nuclear war never far removed, it may well be questioned whether the enormously complex and slow-moving procedures of the American government are adequate to meet both the dangers and opportunities of our foreign relations. Too often, decisions of principle are postponed or neglected and opportunities lost because of the obstacles to decision imposed by our policy processes. The source of this malady is the diffusion of authority between and within the executive and legislative branches and the accessibility of all of these centers of power to a wide variety of pressures and interests. The problem is compounded by the durable myth of Jacksonian democracy, the view that any literate citizen can do almost any job and that a democracy can do without a highly trained administrative elite.

At least since 1917, the ability of the United States to advance its national interests, internally as well as externally, has come to depend upon our ability to cope with world-wide revolutionary forces. These dynamic forces, to understate the matter, have not readily lent themselves to treatment through the leisurely deliberative processes of the American constitutional system. My question is not whether we might *wish* to alter our traditional foreign policy-making procedures but whether in fact we have any choice but to do so in a world that obstinately refuses to conduct its affairs under Anglo-Saxon rules of procedure.

The source of an effective foreign policy under our system is Presidential power. This was never more clear than in the Cuban crisis of October 1962 when decisions of the utmost gravity were made by the President with the assistance of only his most intimate advisers in the executive branch. The circumstances were such that it was quite impossible to seek the counsel of the leaders of Congress, who in fact—and quite properly—were informed but not consulted. Congress had in fact implicitly acknowledged the infeasibility of consultation in an emergency by adopting in the summer of 1962 resolutions authorizing the President to use force if necessary to defend our vital interests in both Cuba and Berlin.

A successful foreign policy for a democracy must be rooted in an informed and responsible national consensus. The achievement of such consensus in the United States is largely, although not entirely, a task of Presidential leadership. The President's voice, Woodrow Wilson said, "is the only national voice in affairs . . . He is the representative of no constituency, but of the whole people. When he speaks in his true character, he speaks for no special interest . . . He is the one person about whom a definite national opinion is formed and, therefore, the one person who can form opinion by his own direct influence and act upon the whole country at once."[29]

There are major areas of foreign policy, those relating more to long-term problems than to immediate crises, wherein Presidential authority is incommensurate with Presidential responsibility as a result of the diffusion of power between executive and legislative branches and within the latter. The foreign policy powers of Congress under the Constitution enable it to implement, modify, or thwart the President's proposals but not itself to initiate or shape policy. These powers, moreover, are widely dispersed within Congress among autonomous committees, each under a chairman who owes little if anything in the way of political obligation to the President.

The defects of Congress as an institution reflect the defects of classical democratic thought. These pertain primarily to foreign policy. In domestic matters, it seems to me, the Congress is as well qualified to shape policy as the Executive, and in some respects more so because of the freedom of at least some members from the particular electoral pressures that operate on the President. The frequency of elections and the local orientation of party organizations, however, do not encourage serious and sustained study of international relations. Congressmen are acutely susceptible to local and regional pressures and to the waves of fear and emotion that sometimes sweep over public opinion. The legislator, in short, is under constant and intense pressure to adhere to the prevailing tendencies of public opinion, however temporary and unstable.

Public opinion must be educated and led if it is to bolster a wise and effective foreign policy. This is pre-eminently a task for Presidential leadership because the Presidential office is the only one under our constitutional system that constitutes a forum for education and political leadership on a national scale. Accordingly, I think that we must contemplate the further enhancement of Presidential authority in foreign affairs. The prospect is a disagreeable and perhaps a dangerous one, but the alternative is immobility and the paralysis of national policy in a revolutionary world, which can only lead to consequences immeasurably more disagreeable and dangerous.

The pre-eminence of Presidential responsibility is in no way an implied license for the legislator to evade national and international responsibility and to surrender to the pressures of local and parochial interest. I can find no better words to define this responsibility than those of Edmund Burke in his classic statement to his constituents at Bristol in 1774:

"Certainly, gentlemen, it ought to be the happiness and glory of a representative, to live in the strictest union, the closest correspondence, and the most unreserved communication with his constituents. Their wishes ought to have great weight with him; their opinion high respect; their business unremitted attention. It is his duty to sacrifice his repose, his pleasures, his satisfactions, to theirs; and, above all, ever, and in all cases, to prefer their interest to his own.

But, his unbiased opinion, his mature judgment, his enlightened conscience, he ought not to sacrifice to you; to any man, or to any set of men living. These he does not derive from your pleasure; no, nor from the law and the constitution. They are a trust from Providence, for the abuse of which he is deeply answerable. Your representative owes you, not his industry only, but his judgment; and he betrays, instead of serving you, if he sacrifices it to your opinion."[30]

As a freshman Senator in 1946 I attempted in a speech at the University of Chicago to define the proper role of the legislator in relation to his constituents, to the nation, and to his own conscience. After seventeen years I see no reason to alter the views I then expressed in these words:

"The average legislator, early in his career, discovers that there are certain interests, or prejudices, of his constituents which are dangerous to trifle with. Some of these prejudices may not be of fundamental importance to the welfare of the Nation, in which case he is justified in humoring them, even though he may disapprove. The difficult case is where the prejudice concerns fundamental policy affecting the national welfare. A sound sense of values, the ability to discriminate between that which is of fundamental importance and that which is only superficial is an indispensable qualification of a good legislator. As an example of what I mean, let us take the poll-tax issue and isolationism. Regardless of how persuasive my colleagues or the national press may be about the evils of the poll tax, I do not see its fundamental importance, and I shall follow the views of the people of my state. Although it may be symbolic of conditions which many deplore, it is exceedingly doubtful that its abolition will cure any of our major problems. On the other hand, regardless of how strongly opposed my constituents may prove to be to the creation of, and participation in, an ever stronger United Nations Organization, I could not follow such a policy in that field unless it becomes clearly hopeless . . ."

We have been compelled by the great historical changes of the twentieth century to qualify the unlimited optimism of classical democratic thought about the relationship of the citizen to government, and we may find it necessary in the foreseeable future to translate this changed perspective into significant alterations in traditional American policy-making procedures. We must at the same time retain and renew our conviction that the core of classical democratic thought, the belief in the moral sanctity of the free mind and the free individual, remains the most valid of human philosophies. In Carl Becker's words: ". . . although we no longer have the unlimited and solvent backing of God or nature, we are still betting that freedom of the mind will never disprove the proposition that only through freedom of the mind can a reasonably just society ever be created."[31]

.        .        .

AS WE look about our country, with its great cities and factories and highways, its magnificent mountains, forests, and rivers, our pride is unbounded. But as we read each day of widespread unemployment, of the rapidly rising crime rate, of increasing juvenile delinquency, we surely cannot but be ashamed of the degradation of so many of our people. The dismal slums in our great cities, the intolerable traffic jams, and the almost universal absence of beauty in our buildings surely must raise some doubt about the manner in which we put to use the enormous energies of our people and the vast wealth generated by our economy. How can it be that a land so blessed by nature has allowed its streams to become polluted, its cities to become blighted and congested, and so many of its citizens to be unemployed and, in truth, to a great extent unemployable because of mental or physical deficiency? In our search for an answer to these questions, we come back inevitably to education, and to the fact that in America it is not meeting its responsibilities.

Education and its improvement are long-term endeavors, but there are immediate steps to be taken. The first action which we as citizens may take is to seek a change in the order of priorities which are presented to the Congress. Surely there is an excessive imbalance in a federal budget which allocates 62 percent of the taxpayers' money to defense and space, 6 percent to the agricultural economy, 6 percent to benefits for war veterans, and 10 percent to interest on a national debt consisting largely of the costs of old wars, leaving only 16 percent for everything else—for public welfare and for all the things that make America a better place in which to live, among which education is counted for an insignificant pittance. This allocation of priorities, in my opinion, is a recipe for disaster, an unrecognized but powerful endorsement of the wrong side in the race between education and catastrophe.

We have reached a juncture in our history at which we must decide whether wealth and power are to be ends in themselves or instruments for the improvement of our lives and our civilization. "Democracy is on trial," said

William James over fifty years ago, "and no one knows how it will stand the ordeal. . . . What its critics now affirm is that its preferences are inveterately for the inferior. . . . Vulgarity enthroned and institutionalized, elbowing everything superior from the highway, this, they tell us, is our irremediable destiny. . . ."[32]

What are the avenues toward excellence and creativity for a democratic society? Surely they are not to be found in the vulgarities of television and mass advertising, in the trivial and mediocre occupations which engage so much of the leisure time of America. Nor are they to be found in some glorious adventure, in the mindless quest for power that destroyed the civilization of ancient Greece and brought ruin to modern Germany. If America is to achieve excellence in life and greatness in history, these can only come from the decision of our people to find purpose and direction in their lives, to give shape and coherence to their civilization. With the leisure and the wealth we have attained, it is open to us to direct some part of our energies to literature and philosophy, to the liberal and the fine arts, to the cultivation of beauty and serenity in our lives. To do these things is to seek meaning in freedom and to secure it as well, because, as August Heckscher has written, "The secret of freedom is courage. And the secret of courage may turn out, after all, to be happiness."[33]

These, I believe, are some of the critical issues on the American agenda. All of them, in one way or another, are the product of the most successful and impressive experiment in nation-building in the history of the world. Honestly approached by a vigorous and ingenious people, they are likely to be resolved, adding thereby to the strength of

America and to the prospects of America for attaining a new plateau of civilization.

These problems of our internal life have everything to do with our prospects at home and everything to do with our prospects abroad—with our hopes for the forging of a concert of free nations and for the ultimate resolution of our conflict with the Communist world. Whether and how we resolve them, far more than our effort to reach the moon, and more even than the course of events in Berlin and Cuba and the jungles of southeast Asia, will have a decisive bearing on the prospects for the West.

*NOTES · INDEX*

# NOTES

## CHAPTER 1: RUSSIA AND THE WEST

1. Edward Gibbon, *The Decline and Fall of the Roman Empire* (New York: Fred DeFau & Co., 1907), IX, 84–85.

2. Speech at Onesti, Rumania, June 20, 1962. "Khrushchev Says No Magician Could Save 'Dying' Capitalism," *New York Times,* June 21, 1962.

3. "The Sources of Soviet Conduct," by "X," *Foreign Affairs,* July 1947, pp. 572–573.

4. Quoted in David J. Dallin, *Soviet Foreign Policy After Stalin* (Philadelphia: J. B. Lippincott, 1961), p. vi.

5. George F. Kennan, *Russia and the West under Lenin and Stalin* (Boston: Little, Brown, 1960), p. 191.

6. Urie Bronfenbrenner, "America's Most Dangerous Prejudice," May 18, 1962, prepared for "The Needs and Images of Man," a conference held at Marquette University, May 1962.

7. Milovan Djilas, *Conversations with Stalin* (New York: Harcourt, Brace & World, 1962), p. 190.

8. *Ibid.,* p. 114.

9. Nikita Khrushchev, "On Peaceful Coexistence," *Foreign Affairs,* October 1959, p. 15.

10. Walter Lippmann, "Soviet-American Relations Today," *Washington Post,* Feb. 13, 1962.

11. Stalin, *Problems of Leninism* (Moscow: Foreign Language Publishing House, 1953), p. 107.

12. Kennan, *Russia and the West,* p. 223.

13. Djilas, *Conversations with Stalin,* p. 114.

14. *Pravda,* April 29, 1958. Quoted in Dallin, *Soviet Foreign Policy After Stalin,* p. 529.

15. Walter Lippmann, address to Women's National Press Club, *Washington Post,* Jan. 11, 1962.

16. Lord Newton, *Lord Landsdowne: A Biography* (London: Macmillan, 1929), p. 467.

17. Raymond Aron, "Coexistence: The End of Ideology," *Partisan Review,* Spring 1958, p. 230.

18. Woodrow Wilson, address at Manchester, England, Dec. 30, 1918. *The Public Papers of Woodrow Wilson: War and Peace,* Ray Stannard Baker and William E. Dodd, eds. (New York: Harper, 1927), I, 351.

## CHAPTER 2:   A CONCERT OF FREE NATIONS

1. Alexis de Tocqueville, *Democracy in America,* translated by Henry Reeve (London: Oxford University Press, 1947), I, 285.

2. George Lichtheim, *The New Europe* (New York: Frederick A. Praeger, 1963), p. 8.

3. Walter Hallstein, *United Europe* (Cambridge, Mass.: Harvard University Press, 1962), p. 29.

4. See John Brooks, "The Common Market," *The New Yorker,* Sept. 22, 1962.

5. Walter Lippmann, "On Not Fidgeting," *Washington Post,* Feb. 21, 1963.

6. Lord Crathorne, "NATO and European Unity," *Parliamentary Debates,* House of Lords Official Report, Feb. 13, 1963, p. 988.

7. Robert Endicott Osgood, *NATO: The Entangling Alliance* (Chicago: University of Chicago Press, 1962), p. 353.

8. G. McKee Rosen, *The Combined Boards of the Second World War* (New York: Columbia University Press, 1951), p. 272.

9. Count Mensdorff, quoted in Harold Nicolson, *Diplomacy,* 2nd ed. (London: Oxford University Press, 1955), p. 141.

10. Alastair Buchan, "The Reform of NATO," *Foreign Affairs,* January 1962, p. 175.

11. Roy Price, *The Political Future of the European Community* (London: John Marshbank, 1962), p. 20.

12. *Problems and Trends in Atlantic Partnership I* (Senate Document no. 132, 1962), p. 30.

13. Walter Lippmann, "Bland and Cheery Words," *Washington Post,* March 7, 1963.

14. Lawrence B. Krause, "The European Economic Community and American Agriculture," in *Factors Affecting the United States Balance of Payments,* Joint Economic Committee, United States Congress (1962), p. 131.

15. Tocqueville, *Democracy in America,* II, 599.

16. Pat M. Holt, Consultant, United States Senate Committee on Foreign Relations, "Nonintervention," unpublished memorandum, Dec. 29, 1961.

17. Report to the President of the United States from the Committee to Strengthen the Security of the Free World, *The Scope and Distribution of United States Military and Economic Assistance Programs* (Department of State, 1963), p. 1.

18. *Ibid.*, p. 4.

19. Walter Lippmann, "The Clay Report," *Washington Post,* March 26, 1963.

20. Robert H. Heilbroner, *The Great Ascent* (New York: Harper & Row, 1963), p. 181.

21. Eric Hoffer, *The Ordeal of Change* (New York: Harper & Row, 1963), pp. 98–99.

22. Heilbroner, *The Great Ascent,* p. 175.

23. Lord Franks, "Cooperation Is Not Enough," *Foreign Affairs,* October 1962, p. 33.

24. Address of Eugene R. Black to the Board of Governors of the World Bank, Washington, Sept. 18, 1962, pp. 13–14.

## CHAPTER 3: THE AMERICAN AGENDA

1. Kenneth W. Thompson, *Christian Ethics and the Dilemmas of Foreign Policy* (Durham, N.C.: Duke University Press, 1959), p. 707.

2. Eric Hoffer, *The Ordeal of Change* (New York: Harper & Row, 1963), p. 40.

3. August Heckscher, *The Public Happiness* (New York: Atheneum, 1962), p. 231.

4. Baruch de Spinoza, "Of Superstition," *The Philosophy of Spinoza* (New York: Modern Library, 1927), p. 3.

5. William Graham Sumner, *What Social Classes Owe to Each Other* (New Haven, Conn.: Yale University Press, reprint of 1925), p. 127.

6. Edward T. Chase, "Learning To Be Unemployable," *Harper's,* April 1963, p. 33.

7. *Ibid.*, p. 40.

8. Horace Mann, *The People Shall Judge* (Chicago: University of Chicago Press, reprint of 1940), pp. 593–594.

9. Quoted in Robert M. Hutchins, *The Conflict in Education* (New York: Harper, 1953), p. 69.

10. Letter to Colonel Charles Yancey, Jan. 6, 1816, *The Writings of Jefferson*, Paul Leicester Ford, ed. (New York: G. P. Putnam's Sons, 1899), X, 4.

11. H. G. Rickover, *Swiss Schools and Ours: Why Theirs Are Better* (Boston: Little, Brown, 1962), p. 19.

12. See Nicholas DeWitt, "Education and the Development of Human Resources: Soviet and American Effort," in *Dimensions of Soviet Economic Power*, studies prepared for the Joint Economic Committee, Congress of the United States (1962), part IV, *The Development of Human Resources*, pp. 233–268.

13. Ralph Barton Perry, *Realms of Value* (Cambridge, Mass.: Harvard University Press, 1954), p. 431.

14. *Further Extracts from the Notebooks of Samuel Butler*, A. T. Bartholomew, ed. (London: Jonathan Cape Press, 1934), p. 120.

15. Hutchins, *The Conflict in Education*, p. 13.

16. Washington's first annual message to Congress, Jan. 8, 1790, *Messages & Papers of the Presidents*, James D. Richardson, ed. (New York: Bureau of National Literature, Inc., 1897), I, 58.

17. Daniel J. Boorstin, "American Nationalism and the Image of Europe, 1914–1945," paper read before the Mississippi Valley Historical Association, April 22, 1954.

18. Louis Hartz, *The Liberal Tradition in America* (New York: Harcourt, Brace & World, 1955).

19. Lewis Mumford, *The City in History* (New York: Harcourt, Brace & World, 1961), p. 550.

20. *Ibid.*, p. 548.

21. "Off the Track: I." *Washington Post*, April 3, 1963.

22. Mumford, *The City in History*, p. 4.

23. *Ibid.*, p. 575.

24. Alexis de Tocqueville, *Democracy in America*, translated by Henry Reeve (London: Oxford University Press, 1947), I, 234–235.

25. Carl L. Becker, *Freedom and Responsibility in the American Way of Life* (New York: Alfred A. Knopf, 1945), p. 32.

26. Walter Lippmann, *The Public Philosophy* (New York: Mentor Books, 1956), pp. 19–27.

27. Quoted by Seth P. Tillman in *Anglo-American Relations at*

*the Paris Peace Conference of* 1919 (Princeton, N.J.: Princeton University Press, 1961), pp. 241–242.

28. Gabriel Almond, *The American People and Foreign Policy* (New York: Harcourt, Brace, 1950), p. 143.

29. Woodrow Wilson, *Constitutional Government in the United States* (New York: Columbia University Press, 1908), pp. 68, 127.

30. *The Works of Edmund Burke* (Boston: Little, Brown, 1897), II, 95.

31. Becker, *Freedom and Responsibility*, p. 42.

32. William James, *Memories and Studies* (New York: Longmans, Green & Co., 1934), p. 316.

33. Heckscher, *The Public Happiness*, p. ix.

# INDEX